How Shall We Train The Child?

Plain talk to parents, particularly mothers, on Christian training in the home

by
Annie Elizabeth Torrance

Wipf and Stock Publishers
150 West Broadway • Eugene OR 97401

How Shall We Train the Child?
by Annie Elizabeth Torrance

Copyright T.F. Torrance, 1996
ISBN: 1-57910-025-2

Printed by WIPF & STOCK PUBLISHERS *1998*

To my dear children

Family Appreciation

It is more than thirty-seven years since our mother wrote this account of how she felt that Christian people should bring up their children. It was written in the year that our father died. They had both answered the call to be missionaries in China and were sent to western Sichuan where they met and were married in 1911. Father was Scots, and mother was English. They were given a family of six children, three girls and three boys, Mary, Tom, Grace, Margaret, James and David, born in that order. James and David arrived several years after the others. Ours was always a very happy life. Our early days were spent in dangerous times and trying circumstances in the aftermath of the Sun Yat Sen revolution when law and order seemed to break down all over China. We lived and went to a school for missionaries' children in Chengdu the capital city of Sichuan, most of whom were Canadian or American, but there was a sprinkling of Europeans. During the summer months we lived in the mountains about forty miles away where we hoped to escape not only from the dusty heat of the plains, but from the malaria, cholera, typhoid, dysentery, and several other enteric diseases that were rife in the cities. We lived during the period when rival warlords fought each other for control of cities and territories and the revenue it could bring. Communist agitators increased steadily inflaming the schools and colleges with their anti-foreign propaganda, and the life of the missionaries was far from being easy. Many were harassed and some of them were killed. These were not circumstances which made it easy to bring up children, but they did have the effect of throwing into sharp relief faith in the saving grace and providential care of the Lord, when Bible study and prayer meant very much to us all. In the face of hardship and danger faith became very much alive. As my father's missionary life involved not a little travel, my mother shouldered a great deal of the responsibility for our daily life.

Our parents, with four of us children, went on furlough for nine months in 1920. In 1927 all of us, now with two younger brothers, returned to Scotland. This time we had been ordered by our consular authorities to leave West China as life under the conflicting military forces, with the rise of communist, nationalist and bandit forces, threatened the existence of foreigners, particularly of missionaries. After a few months at home our parents came to the decision that father should return to Sichuan to continue his missionary work, while mother should remain at home with the family. It was a difficult and painful decision for father to be separated from his wife and family for another seven years, and for mother to be separated from father and to bring her own missionary activity in China to an end. Neither she nor father liked the idea of sending us to boarding schools or of asking relatives to take care of us. Mother felt deeply that it belonged to her missionary calling to see us through our schooling and university education, and to continue her teaching and training of us in the Christian faith and life. This meant that she had rather more to do with us through our early years than my father, although he kept in regular touch with us every week through his letters to my mother and to us children. It was in these circumstances, in China and in Scotland, that she developed the ideas about bringing up children, which she was often urged to communicate in a form that might be helpful to others. Our mother certainly practised in love and understanding what she preached. All of us owe her an immeasurable debt for the way she brought us up, and trained us in the Christian way of life and belief. We learned later in life that father and mother had dedicated each of us to the Lord and his service before we were born. It was a joy to them that all their children were committed to Christ. Each of us in different ways answered the call of the Lord Jesus in the service of the Gospel, and tried to raise our own children in the way we ourselves had been brought up.

Now many years after our mother wrote this little work, people who knew about it have been asking again and again that it should be made readily available through publication, not least in view of the fact that family structure and life have come under increasing attack, and relations between parents and their children have been seriously corroded in the social pathology of our times. At first we thought that what she had written should be given a more up-to-date form, and be pruned of repetition. But we decided that it would be best to leave it more or less as it came from our mother's pen, for it has a distinctive warmth and charm and a spiritual thrust which we felt should not be allowed to be blunted or get lost through our editing. It is now sent forth in this printed form with the prayer that it may help other parents in the Christian training of their children, and help children on their part to understand something of the deep moral and religious issues that are involved in the life and structure of the human family and the Christian way of life in obedience to the teaching of the Bible.

The Torrances, November, 1996

CONTENTS

Preface xiii

1. A Two-Fold Gift: the Child 1
2. Acknowledging the Gift 15
3. Early Years 29
4. Pre-School Years 43
5. The Place of God and His Word in the home 57
6. First Years at School - Readjustment 75
7. The Teenage - Comrades 93
8. The Straying Sheep - Faith Undaunted 115

Preface

This is an attempt to put into writing some of the things discussed in addresses, and also answers to questions raised by Christian parents who are concerned about the spiritual growth of their children in these difficult days. I have tried to write in an informal way, following the informal pattern of the talks given; suggesting and passing on ways that have been helpful and practised by some. At the same time there is no wish to be dogmatic, for as individuals differ so much from each other, especially in character, temperament and sensibility, so children have to be considered personally, even those in one family.

It has been suggested from time to time that something might be put into permanent form along this line. However, there never seemed to be time for this, and perhaps the urge to do so was not there. Lately, however, the suggestion from more than one quarter was made again and it seemed that the right time had arrived to make the effort. I am conscious of how inadequate it is but I derive some encouragement from the memory of many loving mothers who have patiently listened to me on various occasions. Their fellowship has meant more to me than they can possibly know, and also their inspiration.

As I have pondered over some of the hard facts that parents are sometimes called to face I have thought of not a few, some known to me personally, who have hidden griefs, and unspeakable burdens to bear and carry. There are also some whose griefs and sorrows cannot be hidden; and those whose hearts are anxious over the way of life their young folk seem likely to choose. These sorrows cannot but stir our hearts and compel us, not only to sympathise, but to share their hardships, with understanding and love. We are all one family in the Lord, and when one suffers, all the children suffer too, and are constrained to bear one another's burdens. As long as we are in the world we are all exposed to the attacks of the Enemy in one form or another, both from without and from within. God has most graciously given us the precious gift of the fellowship of saints and of those who understand; even though no word may be spoken. The Holy Spirit, in His own way communicates the sorrows, heart-breaks, and anxieties, from each to the other in time of need, as well as the call for the comfort and love of His family.

I am greatly indebted to my own children. I owe more to them than I can ever express. I have learned from them very much in every way and not least the Christian way of life. They will recognise, may be, that all that is written within these pages has not always been practised by me at all times. I have learned much in later years that I could wish I had known in the earlier ones. I am sure many will understand this and have a fellow feeling. For all the help of my children and friends among whom I have ministered I do feel deeply grateful.

I am conscious that there is much that could be said, and might have been said. It was difficult to decide whether certain things should be included or not, but I felt that the main thing was to keep the spiritual goal always to the fore. If that were so, many of the other things would naturally find a solution. Perhaps someone else will take up the trail where this comes short; but in the meantime may there be some crumbs of help to others, however small, which God will graciously use in preparing His own for His Kingdom and service. Nothing can be of value or use that does not come from Him.

A.E.T. Edinburgh, 1959

1

*A Two-Fold Gift:
the Child*

Few moments of more unspeakable joy can come to anyone during a lifetime than that moment when a new born babe is laid in a mother's arms for the first time! The days of patient waiting, of fortitude, sometimes with much weariness, with its climax of pain and fear are soon forgotten in that wonderful moment! Hope at last has given place to possession. How the horizon has changed for both parents! With the birth of a first child there seems to be a kind of re-birth of the parents. Certainly there is a sense of maturity - of having arrived; and a new feeling of responsibility, not known before. Here is a helpless, clinging babe utterly dependent on the love and care of his or her parents. New determinations, new emotions and hopes crowd into the heart and mind. What belonged to the past now seems trivial and sinks away into the background. Life has become bigger and a much more important place to live in. There is a new objective and something to aspire to. The cry of the babe, the touch of its hand, the gentle gaze from its sleepy eyes are like new wine to the parents and life seems to have acquired wings!

Yet is this all? Is it enough? Surely behind all the natural joy and deep down in the heart are there not questions that come to the surface? To Christian parents there must be. What kind of man or woman will this small babe become one day? Here is not only a new born babe, but a living soul, an eternal creation. Here is something far more profound, and of far greater consequence than appears to the eye. A little seed: into what will it grow? Wrapped up in this little bundle of life are the beginnings of all that will one day reach maturity, whether for good or ill: characteristics, emotions, prejudices, the power to choose or reject, to scorn or to love, the beginning of those things that make life harder or easier for others to live in the world. "We spend our life like a tale that is told", and in this life it has a beginning and an end. It is the beginning of a tiny new life like a silvery stream that trickles out of the rocks on the hillside, and flows down into a bubbling brook, but as it goes on its course, it gathers strength and speeds its way into the sea - but which sea?

Let us think of the Babe that was born to Mary in Bethlehem. Who would ever have dreamed that the Eternal Son of God would come into the world as a helpless babe and into the arms of a lowly Hebrew maid? How dimly could Mary apprehend in that hour that she held in her arms the Saviour of the world! The angel, the annunciation, the worship and the witness of the shepherds, the adoration of the wise men and the splendour of the Star that appeared over the cattle stall that night in Bethlehem must have filled the breast of Mary with a strange joy and wonder. Yet, when the time came for them to take the babe into the temple in Jerusalem to present Him to the Lord, the aged Simeon also came into the Temple, to whom God had revealed His precious secret. Taking the Babe up in his arms he blessed and thanked God for the Heaven-Sent Child; but turning to Mary he said, "This child is set for the rise and fall of many and a sign that will be spoken against". "Yea", he said, "a sword will pierce through your soul also that the thoughts of many hearts may be revealed." How strange those words must have sounded to Mary in the midst of her joy. No doubt she understood when she stood at the foot of the Cross, and her own soul was indeed pierced with unspeakable sorrow, as she saw the nail-torn hands and the pierced side of God's Lamb as He hung on the Cross.

How symbolic was Mary's experience of joy and sorrow, love and pain! How in a far less way does it come to us all! For some reason, partly hidden from us now, we do have to pass through the vale of sorrow and tears, for it is part of the pathway that leads to Him. Yet He comforts us along the way with His promise that "God will wipe away all tears from our eyes and there will be no more death, neither sorrow or any more pain, for these things will pass away". The writer of the hymn expresses it thus,

> *All our life is touched with pain,*
> *And shadows fall on brightest hours,*
> *And thorns remain.*

The Holy Babe came to Mary as God's pure Gift imparted to her from above and beyond herself altogether - the unspeakable Gift to us all. For the Christian, most things have a spiritual counterpart, a shadow of the Divine Truth contained in the things we handle and see. Hence in a humbler way the birth of a little child on earth reminds us that it is truly a gift from God. A little babe is laid in our arms, a visible token of what He, the Strong Son of God, was once, now the Victorious, Risen Lord.

And this new and wonderful joy that comes to us in the arrival of the babe also brings with it a measure of awe, not untouched with fear. Yet this is fear that is wholesome because it is joined to hope, which makes us seek the Lord that we may rely on Him for all the wisdom that we need in order to do all that He would have us do with His precious gift.

In considering the gift of life let us now look at it in another way. The inventions and creations of man are truly marvellous in our day. We have gone from one discovery to another. In search for knowledge man has touched and raised terrible possibilities. He has reached out after the great dynamic forces that govern the universe and seeks to harness them either for the welfare and comfort of the human race, or, on the other hand, to hasten the destruction of the world. Humanity is moved with fear and apprehension lest these mighty forces in and under the earth and above the earth should get beyond man's control, or be used in the rage of man against man. But the Christian has little to fear, for after all, man is still limited. He cannot create life; he may cripple and distort it, but he cannot create it. That is the sole prerogative of the Prince and Author of Life. Thus the new-born babe defies all men's inventions. He or she is a living, tangible, witness to the Son of God that "All things were made by Him, and without Him was not anything made that was made". Yes, this new-born babe is life. This is God's own gift. In him or her God has touched the earth with life. We may have hoped, longed and prayed for this little one, but only God can breathe the life of the child into our midst.

We may be stirred by man's inventions, but how much greater is the babe we hold in our arms! Whether we realise it or not, this new life is quite wonderful, something which the parents claim as theirs and yet something that is too great for their comprehension. It is God's gift of life. It is a life that is meant to increase and grow, affecting in some way or other all it contacts, fulfilling its course in this world and the next. Our Lord says, "I am come to give life and to give it more abundantly."

If this little life has been given to us as God's creation and gift, then without doubt there comes with it a meaning and purpose in the Divine Will. It has been remarked that God is always economical in all things. He never creates to waste. For example, God said "Let the earth bring forth grass, the herb yielding fruit after its kind whose seed is in itself". There was to be the increase, the use, the law and the goal. To human beings life must remain a mystery until God lifts the veil. "We see through a glass darkly, as in a riddle"; some day we will see His Face and then we shall know. The main thing for those of us who believe and hope for eternal life with Christ our Lord, is that we reflect upon the fact that there is a spiritual meaning and definite purpose of God in this little child as well as a destiny which we must keep in mind. God has given a two-fold gift, a human life to love and cherish, and a living soul to teach, train and bring to the Great Shepherd, out of whose hand none shall pluck them.

Our temptation is to forget and lose sight of the main issues. We are carried away and absorbed with things seen. Even the best of Christian parents become so taken up with the common necessities that sometimes God just isn't counted in with the care of the child as he should be. The child is a joy and is meant to be, and the days are fully occupied with things necessary for the child. We delight in every new sign of development and intelligence, while the demands for the well-being of the child absorb our time and thought. But sometimes our joy may become a concern and worry as we get into difficulties. At such times God would remind us that when He gives his gifts, He gives Himself with them. God is always so different from us. His ways are so much higher than ours. When we give gifts to one another, we are apt to spoil them by being conscious of ourselves, and thrust ourselves before our gifts, allowing our motives to be mixed up even though we may not be conscious of it ourselves. Unlike this, God seems to hide Himself in the shadow, for He covets our love and our hearts, not for what He gives but for what He is and desires. It is rather like a parent who has set his heart on some special gift for his child, perhaps at Christmas. When the time arrives the father presents the gift to his child and then silently watches to see what the child will do, whether he is pleased and appreciates the gift or not. We all know the joy when a child shows he is conscious of the love and thought of his parent, even as he welcomes the gift.

  A charming story comes to mind of an occasion when a new born babe arrived into a family of boys and girls. The father went off to tell the glad news to the other children. "Oh", said one of the little girls, "Does Mummy know about it?" The child wanted to share her joy at once with the one whom she loved. Does not God wait for us to share our joy with Him though He is the Giver of the joy? The important thing is that we do acknowledge His guidance and council. So much depends on our doing this from the beginning. God in His wonderful way gives us so much freedom along with all our other opportunities. It is perhaps because of this that we delay and postpone things that ought to be done much earlier. In after years how many parents have sore hearts and anguish of spirit over the child that was once so lovely and such a joy and delight. Of course there may be many reasons why that may happen, but one perhaps is that the start was not right. If only we could guard against our proneness to be slack and negligent. The Preacher in Ecclesiastes was not out of the way when he said, "To everything there is a season, and a time to every purpose." To buy up the opportunity at the right time before it is too late, is certainly the wisest plan. To most of us come many possibilities, though even they may seem so small that we are likely to make little of them, waiting for the bigger things to come along, which in all probability will elude us. Too often we run along in the busy thoroughfare of our daily life not heeding the red lights of warning that call us to stop and think. Many an older man and woman, looking back over the years has been filled with sadness and regret. "If only I had done differently, been more patient and considerate, more alive to the possibilities that once were mine, how different things might have been now." In God's eyes nothing is impossible and nothing hopeless. He knows our regrets and in His Love; He heals and forgives, and adds yet more grace, by restoring "the years that the locusts have eaten". The care of the young infant is certainly something we can do for God. Some parents appear to regard their baby as a kind of toy and novelty; others take the birth of the child as an ordinary affair of life and one of those things we have to have and accept. To appropriate some words from the Holy Scriptures, "Take this child and nurse it for me, and I will give you wages." We cannot forget what the Lord of the vineyard said to the one who had neglected what had been given to him. "What hast thou done with what I gave you?" Let us be sure then that we ponder over and consider that this precious little life is truly the gift of the Life-Giver. This does not refer to that supernatural life of which our Lord spoke to Nicodemus, but to the natural life that God gives to us all when we come into the world and which is meant to be the portal into the eternal life which we may enjoy with Him through our Lord Jesus.

We love the springtime when the trees burst into new life, and the flowers spring out of the dead earth, the birds awake us to nature's call and swell their throats with their love-songs. All life awakens after the long death-like winter. It is a symbol of spiritual things, the witness to all that God lives, and is still at His creating work. The little babe as it unfolds, stretches its limbs and opens its eyes, is no less a witness of God's thought and love. Nothing is an end in itself but reaches out to the everlasting things. The children that God sends to us are in His purpose to inherit that eternal life which God has purchased for all who believe. The natural life in the babe is meant to find its fullness and reality in Him who is the Eternal Life. The gifts that God gives are never meant to be used selfishly on ourselves or for our own ends. In God's economy they are to bear fruit in the glory of His creation.

St Paul says, "We are not our own, we have been bought with a price." These things are not only true of ourselves as Christians, but equally of the babe whom God has committed to our charge. It is life which God expects to be rendered back to Him, life through which He can demonstrate His great Love, and which will, because of Him, be fragrant and fruitful and lovely in His sight. Therefore we are not only the parents but caretakers of God's property. God has called us into His special service through this child. He has made us His co-partners, to share with Him the joy of His salvation, which He has purchased for all mankind in the bringing in of His everlasting Kingdom. We are thus honoured with God's trust to us in which lie great possibilities and God's desire for the child.

It is for our comfort and peace that we recall these things soon, and accept what God has committed to our charge, as from Himself. Then no matter what may lie ahead, we shall at all times be able to turn to Him who is the Source of all knowledge and understanding. The baby's needs will increase each day and our need of wisdom and strength will also increase, as our responsibility becomes more manifest to ourselves. We all feel our insufficiency, and God means it to be so that we may the more readily cast ourselves on Him. We remember how Moses, even when weighed down with rebellious Israel in the wilderness, cried out to the Lord that the burden was too great for him, and no doubt that was part of God's plan for Moses that he might know that he was unable to carry out God's commission to him alone. God's answer is ever inspiring to us all when we get up against things, for God speedily answered him by sending the Angel of His Presence to be with him throughout their journeyings. That Rock which followed them, as St Paul says, was Christ, and Moses himself from that time was strengthened into a rock-like nature that was able to bear without flinching or faltering the mighty burden unto the end.

The novelty of our babe will wear away but the reality will remain, and joy in the possession of our little one will be intensified if we have the conscious companionship of the Lord every step of the way. God will allow us to feel our need of Him in times of sickness, anxiety, distress and trial, from which none of us can escape. As parents we need Him more than ever. The little child needs Him too, though so small, and it is through the parent that the babe's need must be met. So much that will necessarily follow later, depends on this right attitude at the start with God, if we are in earnest about our child's spiritual welfare and salvation.

The Jews looked upon children as God's gift to them. Children were the sign of His favour and blessing. We have many examples of this in the Old Testament Scriptures. We remember how Isaac was withheld until Abraham and Sarah were old. Sarah had waited many long years for this sign of blessing and promise which was also to be a sign of the greater spiritual blessings to come. We think of the bitterness of Rachel and her long wait for Joseph, after which God added blessing to blessing in Israel through her son. We remember the mother of Samuel who sought for a child with tears and prayer. In the New Testament we read how Zecharias' prayer of many years concerning the barrenness of his wife Elizabeth was answered at last, although none must have been as shattered as his wife, who was too old to have a child. But as Elizabeth said, "the Lord has taken away my reproach" - John the Baptist was given to them with all the additional joy of the blessed Hope of the coming of Christ, the Promised One. These holy women knew of the promises made to Abraham and the patriarchs that through the Hebrews God would bring into the world a Saviour who would forgive sins. They were ever expectant that the Royal Line would come through them and their children.

We as Christians can have the same hope that Christ shall be born again in the hearts and souls of our children and hasten the final Coming of the Lord to reign on earth as in heaven. Children ever played a part in the Old Testament. They are mentioned as "the olive branches around the table", or as the pleasant fruit of the vine. When Israel was in captivity and Jerusalem and "the pleasant land" were overthrown and left in heaps because of the sin and rebellion of the people of God, the prophet Zechariah, who was sent to hearten the remnant of true believers, foretold that the people should return to Zion and that "the streets of the city should be full of boys and girls playing in them". These were tokens of peace and love and of God's unfailing care of his own. "He carries the lambs in His bosom". If all this is so precious in God's sight, how much more should we see in our children God's will and design for His Kingdom?

It is a mystery to us all that God should need men and women through whom to show forth His Glory, the works of salvation and the blessedness that shall be hereafter. "Frail children of dust and feeble as frail" - what use can they be to the Holy God who dwells in the Light that no one can approach, who is a consuming fire? In His Presence sin cannot be tolerated, and before Him the greatest of saints have fallen as dead. How, we ask, can this Holy One have any need for such sinful creatures? No doubt it is in His Love that He draws the veil before our eyes lest we should faint and be utterly discouraged. It is His mystery now, but He assures us, "What I do thou knowest not now, but thou shalt know hereafter." He lets us know enough. He satisfies us with good things so that we may run in His paths, and be continually renewed in His strength each day. He has given us "Grace abounding", and revealed to us abundant salvation for our souls, and in His time the redemption of the body. The privilege of serving now is ours. Not to angels has He delegated this holy mystery on earth, but to us He has given angels' work to do for

Him. The Lord has need of us. We read how passionately our Lord spoke to His disciples in St John's Gospel on the eve of his death on the Cross. He was to leave them, a few of His friends, frightened and feeble. They were to carry the story of redemption to all the world against the fiery gates of hell and the devil. But He did not leave them alone. He went with them in the Holy Spirit, and the great work went forward of building the Church His Body. Our Lord poured out His Love upon them. "If any man love me he will keep my words and my father will love him and we will come and make our abode with him."

Can we count it a light thing to be in charge of a living soul? Let us remember that every child born has a soul. Our Lord is the pattern. He came as man, and in the same form as our babe. God has taught us how we should live, work, and honour the Father, and honour the value of human life. When he arose and returned to the Father, He committed this work to the disciples to carry the good news of salvation to the uttermost parts of the earth, and to labour until He returned - just earthen vessels to bear the heavenly treasure. Beyond doubt there might have been other ways for God to work but He chose common men, made of the dust, limited in their apprehension of heavenly things. The Glory of God must ever belong to God alone.

Not only does God need men and women, but boys and girls, according to His Word. He needs them; He wants them. Little children find it so much easier than many adults to come to Him. It is quite natural with them. They turn to Him as the flower turns to the sun. They are His precious jewels, and no doubt feel the drawing power of the Sun of Righteousness. But God expects us to bring them to Him. The new born babe is another life for Him to live in, feet for Him to walk in, hands for Him to use, a voice for Him to speak through, a heart for Him to love through. The babe is God's opportunity in the completion of His work. Our part is to see that He comes into the possession of His own, and that we never attempt to go it alone, but always as workers together with Him. "Apart from me you can do nothing." What shall we render unto the Lord for His unspeakable gift in Christ

Jesus, who came into this world as a helpless babe? Is there a better way than to determine, as far as in us lies, that we train our little one for Him so that He can say of each of our children, "They shall be mine, in the day when I make up my jewels"?

2

Acknowledging the Gift

There is an attractive story recorded in the Book of Judges about a man called Manoah and his wife who apparently had no child. It seems certain that they had prayed that God would bless them in this way, and were certain that God had heard and would answer their prayer. This child was to have a special mission in the Hebrew nation, and though we learn that he missed the mark in some respects, yet his name is recorded in the gallery of those who wrought mightily through faith for God, and whose name is remembered in the Epistle to the Hebrews in the New Testament. The parents were instructed about the child before he was even conceived - which reminds us about how early God works! It is doubtless God's will for us that we should follow this example and prepare the way for our children by prayer and the Word of God. When the parents were told of the work for God that their son was ordained to do, they were deeply impressed and awed. They felt the weight of their responsibility, and their own helplessness. They appear to have been simple country folk, and no doubt blessedly simple in faith. When the angel of God visited them again they asked the question, "How shall we order the child?" How shall we bring him up? They received the answer emphatically that they were to observe very thoroughly all that God had commanded them to do.

There are other stories in the Scriptures that reveal how

important a thing in God's eyes is the child He sends into the world, to be cared for by earthly parents. We remember the story of Hannah and how she prayed that she might have a child; she prayed earnestly with tears and pled with God that He would take away her reproach from among women, as childlessness was reckoned to be among the Hebrew people. God answered her prayer abundantly, and Hannah confirmed her trust in God by dedicating to Him her son. Even before he was born her faith stretched out in firm belief that God would own and use the child she believed He would give. How many of us have sought the Lord as Hannah did? Her gratitude of praise burst into song as she fulfilled her part of her petition, and took her little son, Samuel, to Eli the old priest, in the Temple of the Lord at Shiloh. Her song was the herald of a greater song, the Song of Songs, the Magnificat, which the Virgin Mary sang when the Eternal Son of God was born into the world. Thus the glorious fact came to pass that God had remembered His Word of promise to His servant Abraham and to Israel, that a Saviour should be born. These triumphant Songs are the precious heritage of the Church on earth today, and ever will be. Who is not quickened as they sing the Magnificat of the Virgin Mary inspired by the Holy Spirit?

If it is true that these recorded births were of people especially called saints, they have a message and a pattern for all parents. St Paul reminds us that it is from the Jews that we have received the lively oracles of God, the Testaments, the Prophets, the Gospel and the written Word of God. Among all this we have the teaching of the way they prayed and ordered their children, even the infants. From the earliest days of the Covenant God made with Israel, we find that the children were always made partakers with their parents in God's promises and blessings: "To you and to your children". When they were called to appear before the Lord on special occasions they came with the women and children they had in the Covenant. In this age we are apt to leave children out of the spiritual inheritance which is surely theirs by right from God. In the New Testament we read that Mary, the mother of the Lord, lost no time in bringing her Child up to Jerusalem, "to present

Acknowledging the Gift

Him to the Lord". Even though He was God's own Son, yet He was, according to the custom of the people and God's ordained law, offered to God publicly in the Temple. How it moves us to think of it! Our Lord would have said no doubt, "For thus it behoves us to fulfil all righteousness", as He did later at His Baptism by John. What then shall we do with our children, we who are sinners saved by His grace, and who owe Him so much? Our Lord Himself was always insistent on fulfilling all that the Scriptures said should be done.

Hebrew mothers used to take their children to the Temple, not only to give thanks for God's gift and goodness to them, but also to present their children to the Lord and ask His blessing as they offered their sacrifice in witness to His forgiveness, redemption and salvation. Ought not we also to enter into the same spirit by bringing our children publicly to the Lord, and acknowledging the holy sacrifice of the Lamb of God, who died for all, even for the little children? And by so doing pray that our children may be inheritors of God's promises, through the ministry of their parents, and be owned and taught by Him. The custom of the Hebrews according to God's command was to circumcise their male children. Circumcision was the sign of the covenant that the children belonged to God's chosen people and that they were thereby separated from the nations. Without this sign they were to be counted as outcasts. We know that in the new covenant circumcision now avails nothing and is done away with. All saints are circumcised in Christ in the circumcision of the heart, and they are still His "peculiar people", a people set apart, through whom He carries on the great work of His Kingdom, just as He carried out His work in ancient times through Israel, His chosen servant. While knowing that God can recreate our children in the Holy Spirit, it is right that we should bring them as early as possible, and present them to Him with our earnest and sincere prayers that He will work His mighty Work in their lives and hearts. Christ Himself has said, "Suffer little children to come unto me".

Our Lord ever insisted on public acknowledgment. The

leper was to go to the Temple to show himself to the priest. The possessed man was to return and tell what great things God had done for him. The woman who touched His garment had to acknowledge her need and her healing. Many other incidents reveal the same thing. In God's sight all our public acknowledgments are meant to be a witness to what He has done for us, as well as acts showing our gratitude; our dedications and consecrations are claims to His Blessings and His Presence. In presenting our children to Him publicly we claim His promises for them and proclaim our belief in His Word. Our Christian witness is, alas, often more one of asking than glorifying God's name and witnessing to Him openly.

Perhaps due to the kind of life we are forced to live and the heavy demands on our time, we fall into the temptation to separate spiritual from material things in our daily living. We keep them in separate compartments; yet God's people, the Jews, always sought to be assured that God was their God in everything. They claimed that God was with them and on their side when He gave them the material means of their daily sustenance. It seemed to them to be a sign of the goodness and favour of God toward them. Although the material was often foremost, nevertheless they did not divorce it from the spiritual. We can learn much from them, and to know the reality of God in everything is one of them.

What we say and do continually are outward signs of what we are within. Our characters are formed and expressed by the things we think and frame in our minds. As our Lord said, "That which proceeds from the heart" makes or mars a person. This also affects our children. What we really are will tell on them more quickly that on anyone else. As we minister to them the necessary things of life, we will, however unconsciously, impress ourselves upon them. But it is above all the spiritual life within that will certainly communicate itself to the child, and that is much more important.

It is certainly through the outward expressions of feeling that the personality of the child will be formed. We have to keep in mind that the babe has not just burst in on our lives for our own enjoyment! Our Lord spoke of the joy of the mother when she receives her child, and of how her travail and pain are soon forgotten in her new-found joy. It is surely the compensation of love and our joy will be more lasting and will increase as we share it with our Lord, and seek to let the government of this little life rest on His shoulders, thereby lightening every burden that will come with increased responsibility. To mingle all we do for the child in a practical way with the spiritual will bring about the result we long for. The impression made on the little brain will find a way to the heart. It is not the intention here to offer advice on the best way to lay a good foundation, physically, for the welfare of the child. Many good books are available for that. Here we are concerned with things important to the Christian parent which bear upon the formation of a child's character. Some people think that all spiritual reference in relation to a baby or a very young child should wait until they are older. That would be a grave mistake. It is amazing and revealing to watch a young baby and observe how it indicates its awareness of things. Many years ago I watched a Chinese nurse washing a baby of a few days old. As the process went on, suddenly a dog barked vigorously in the garden. The infant on the lap of the nurse at once moved its head and made a gesture at the noise, and the old nurse who had washed many such babies said, in her broken English, "Ah she savy noise"! Such a baby can "savy" much more than noise. The tiny seeds that are sown early in the spring will with the rain and sunshine lose no time in working away under the soil, and the outer shell will crack and the energy will force up the tiny shoots. See how patiently the gardener watches, until in the right environment the plants develop as he had hoped in the right way and at the right time. So it is with the infant child.

    The inward growth begins as soon as the outward; unseen, it goes on and much will depend on the environment as to the form it will take. The love and gentleness of the parental care lavished on the child will soon show its results. Peace and contentment will shape the expression. A babe hungers by nature for love as much as for food. Love is a language it can understand.

A rough, impatient hand, a nasty spirit, a harsh voice and bad temper will also have its effect on the child. It will become uneasy, restless and fretful, and naturally this has its reaction on its spiritual nature. The harsh east wind blights the sturdiest flower. The mother of a baby of three months was taken seriously ill. The infant had to be given into the charge of another, a nurse well trained in every way. Yet one thing seemed to be missing. The mother's love was not there, and soon what had been a contented, peaceful child became a fretful and crying one. There was ceaseless whining and restlessness which no one seemed to be able to pacify. After several weeks the mother began to get better and the child was brought to her. Could that unhappy face ever be forgotten? With its look of despair, the drooping head looked like a wilted flower. Weeks of love and care brought back the smile, the restful, contented look, and the happy, cooing notes returned.

A story also comes to mind from a missionary in India, in which an elderly Indian lady was being taken round the wards of a children's hospital. One small infant was crying pitifully and it was explained that the child continually cried and no one seemed to be able to find out the reason. She went over to the cot and looked at the baby, then took it up in her arms and folded it to her breast, comforted and soothed it, and the child ceased to cry and changed the expression of its face. "There", she said, "that is what it needs, mother love." Some people think it quite natural for a child to spend a good deal of time crying, but there is generally a reason for its unhappiness, and sometimes it pays to give time and leisure for the "mother love" as the Indian lady said. Nothing makes a baby or a little child happier than the sense that it is loved. It is the air it must breathe in order to thrive. This also has its counterpart in the spiritual life of the soul. Love comes to it from God through the mother, and it will play its part also in satisfying the spirit of the child.

As the mother is, so the child will be. That is her prerogative in the very early years. She has to feed and wash the child, and the mother quite naturally fills the child's horizon. An affinity will continually grow between them, defying words to explain. The child will watch its mother's face and be quick to detect and feel any disturbance there. It will respond to her every mood, and be concerned at every indifference and forgetfulness. A mother, calm and placid, relaxed and contented in mind, will reproduce those qualities in her infant. It is not always easy to realise that our spiritual restfulness and assurance are doing the same for the child. As the Lord makes His face to shine into the heart of the mother, so it will be reflected as in a mirror in the face of the child.

As the child grows and increases in awareness, it naturally draws attention to itself and thereby becomes a temptation to be a source of amusement for the adults. Friends and relations alike try to attract the baby and stimulate its attention. Naturally it responds, but when carried on too long the child is exhausted and gives way to crying. The father may be one of the culprits here! He may have been out all day and comes home and starts a good frolic with his child. The baby is thrown up and down in the air, its eyes turning in all directions and not knowing whether to be afraid or pleased. Sometimes the babe is danced round the room until the parent himself is tired and sinks into a chair, but the babe thus roused up to unusual activity thinks something is wrong when it suddenly stops, and so ends up in a good bout of crying, and the mother, probably tired, has to come to the rescue. This is certainly not the most helpful treatment of the babe. It is a mistake to arouse the mind to mental energy before the physical frame is ready for it. All nature works in harmony, and it is only where there is a lack of balance that things go wrong. Few things work well if there is a lack of balance or disharmony in the machinery. It is true with ourselves. People get nervy, irritable and ill, often because there has been the overtaxing of one part of their body or mind more than another. They have been taxed beyond their strength and what they are able for. This produces the "strain" so many talk about these days. People strive to keep up with all that they think is expected of them, and so often it is quite beyond their powers physical and mental. These things cause breakdowns and nervous collapse. The infant can suffer in the same way. How often a small child gets beyond control when it is a few years old! It is disobedient, defiant, rebellious and fractious about everything, and the parent may give way to spanking or continuous scolding, never realising perhaps that the fault is really with the parents themselves, and that most of this indisposition has been produced in the child's earliest days by wrong treatment. It is in these innumerable daily occurrences that the character and disposition of the child are being formed, although in most cases this is scarcely realised. An infant thrives best in every way if it is left for the most part of its earliest months as quiet as possible. This does not mean that it should not be spoken to in a quiet way and have its times of play. Most mothers use the time when bathing and dressing, particularly towards the end of the day for this little relaxation. But that should really be enough. The babe is continually growing and developing and it is easy to put things out of tune. A babe put out into the fresh air, kept warm, and attended to by its mother, will develop and grow in body and mind in such a way that it will take in its stride with ease and without effort all that in time is demanded of it. If there are clever brains in any child, they will develop normally only if allowed to do so at their own pace. We cannot spur on nature without getting into trouble. The Scriptures say "In quietness and confidence shall be your strength". It is a wise saying for us all, and it is as true in the case of the infant as in that of every one else. To treat a babe or young child in a rowdy way is drastically wrong, for it will likely become a difficult child, and no credit to its parents in after years. Patience is a most valuable asset in us all and not less so when a tiny child is being cared for. It has its own reward and contributes to a happy home. Many people are quick to label a fretful child as ill tempered and try to trace the reason from every source but the right one. In many cases it could be found that the balance between the physical and the mental needs readjusting. Neglected, it may be the cause of many nervous troubles in later life where the right equilibrium has never been perfectly acquired.

    On the other hand, some mothers tend to keep their babies too sheltered from noise. All natural noises about the house are suppressed and the common routine of things is adjusted so as not to disturb the child. In that way the home becomes abnormal and uncomfortable for others who have to live there. It can have a bad effect and produce a nervy, easily startled child. Sooner or later it will have to hear noises and become accustomed to the general activity of daily life. To be quite natural about these things will have the best effect and prepare the little one for a natural way of life. Regularity in everything is a big contribution in making a child well poised and contented. Infants quickly respond to habits. Fixed times for eating, dressing, washing, sleeping, and all else that fits into the daily routine, make the best appeal and get the best results. Things like irregularity can disturb and unsettle an infant. To lapse into the habit of doing things spasmodically does not suit a baby any more than it suits an adult. Eating irregularly and performing other functions of living irregularly affect the digestion and of course the disposition. There are many things that may cut across a good habit-forming routine. Visitors may come, or an engagement unfortunately made for the wrong time, has to be kept. Perhaps a piece of work needs doing or other things charge in and the claims of the child are put aside until there is time! Happy the mother who at all costs keeps her appointments with her child! She will be well rewarded in time.

An even tenor of life gives a child a sense of security and confidence without which it will be unhappy. Security is the desire of all human nature. Even the little dumb creatures seek it, and the babe is no exception. A child is quick to sense when security is there and when it is not. The mother is the key to that in the earlier years, and later on, the father. One can observe many implications of this. An infant when not very well in its parent's arms will sometimes put out its hand to draw the parent's face towards itself, asking for the comforting love it knows to be there, a touching sight which speaks for itself. With understanding as well as love the child will maintain strength, physically, mentally, and spiritually. Seeking to maintain an all-round balance for the well-being of the child will simply repay any sacrifice that has to be made. It will go far to guarantee a healthy body and mind and make spiritual things natural. One is reminded of an orchestral piece of music. Throughout the rendering there is the constant, persistent theme, sometimes soft, sometimes louder, but always underlying or penetrating the various instruments until as the music reaches its climax the theme is united with all the volume of music as it bursts into a perfect harmony and unison of triumph. So the undertone of spiritual possibility is always there waiting to be caught up into the physical and mental, the outward and inward, things that make up life in its fullness. It is this persistent, insistent appeal of the soul's need for its realisation which should not be neglected; without it the heart is unsatisfied and life is meaningless, if not chaotic. Human beings old and young are only at rest in heart when they know that they are right with God and partakers of spiritual life with Him; when all that alienates them from Him has been taken away, and they are in tune with the Infinite. God has made us for Himself and only when we know we have a place in His heart through Jesus Christ, and life is in harmony with Him, can we have courage, hope and peace to face life. In a miniature way this is also reflected in the life and soul even of a child.

It is this atmosphere of spiritual awareness from the beginning that will bring God and His way of salvation into the life of a child in a simple and natural way. Too often it is deferred until the mind and outlook of a child have largely been formed without God, and the effort to bring them to the Lord is harder, because the spiritual sensitivity has been neglected rather than encouraged. The result of neglecting this spiritual aptitude, which God gives to all when they come into the world, is as it would be with any other faculty, indifference, if not impotency. To Christian parents prayer is vital if the right atmosphere is to be maintained. "Pray without ceasing", said St Paul, and again, "continue instant in prayer". Our Lord said also, "that we ought always to pray, and not to faint". Some one said that "prayer is the Christian's vital breath", and it certainly keeps us in touch with all the power we need for daily life. Through prayer we are quickened and made aware of our needs as well as our calling. As John the Baptist went before the Lord to prepare His way, so we, as parents, are called to go before Him and prepare His way to the heart of the child. The nearer we live to God the nearer the child will be. The more we behold the Face of the Father in the Lord Jesus in prayer, the more we shall all be transformed into His likeness and an increase in spiritual consciousness will come to the child. Such little habits of saying grace before meals, and saying prayers, are better begun early even though the child cannot understand much at the time. Little children are quite natural and easy to lead if we are natural too in the things of God, and take them for granted as much as the daily routine. To be truly spiritually minded, as St Paul enjoins, creates around us a God-consciousness which will have its effect on the child. A boy and a girl some time ago wanted to join a church and were interviewed by the minister separately. When asked when they first knew the Lord, they answered that they did not remember when they did not know Him. The minister was a little perturbed and asked the mother, who explained that the Lord Jesus had been a natural part of the home. Those two had known the environment of the Saviour at a very early age. "I, being in the way the Lord led me."

The good habits of daily prayer, reading the Bible and meditating on the Word of God will equip us for this most precious task. Often life seems too demanding, and we are cast down and get physically tired, and the temptation comes to let things go. We give way to self-pity perhaps and the temperature around us drops to freezing point and has its effect on all in our home, including the infant. At such times it is helpful to examine our daily life and see how much time we waste on things that are unnecessary; and how a little re-arrangement of duties, with some self-discipline and self-denial in things which, though quite legitimate and socially attractive, are better forgone for a while that we may conserve strength and time for relaxation for the sake of the babe and the home. It is not infrequent that a Christian mother becomes involved in too many outside activities which take her away from the home and the child too much. But it should be remembered that the infant really has the prior claim on the mother's time in the early years. More time given to the Word of God and letting the Holy Spirit apply it to the need of the heart, are a wonderful tonic. We are quickened by the Word of God, and if we will, we shall find it satisfies beyond all else.

Many people complain of their difficult children in their later years. Perhaps much of this could have been avoided if there had been more time spent and more perseverance in creating a happy spiritual awareness in the home, which would have imprinted itself indelibly on the heart of the child and wound those cords of love around it which none can tear from the memory. Like everything else, if we sow abundantly we shall reap abundantly. It is in our power to create a restful, happy atmosphere for our children which will be a lasting background. We can foster a quiet and natural God-consciousness in our home and an "at-homeness" with the Lord in which not only quite small children will come to know Him, and are easily brought to Him, but an access is opened to Him that will stand in time of need throughout life. Let us make sure we are among those of whom it was said "They brought unto Him also infants", and let us keep on bringing them until they know the way to come themselves.

3

Early Years

One sometimes hears a young couple talk of "settling down to rear a family"! This sounds rather like starting a farm to rear chickens, ducks, etc, and suggests a thorough-going business undertaking. The emphasis, perhaps misunderstood, seems to be laid in the wrong place, and the purpose is not clear. It is certainly not how Christian parents should approach the call to parenthood. To be entrusted with the care and upbringing of a human family demands an altogether different outlook.

To sincere Christians the act of becoming parents is not unlike being commissioned in the army, for they are called into the service of the King of Kings and His Kingdom. The privilege of training, guiding and bringing little children to Him is not just "child's play", and is certainly no light task. There is no "off duty" in this service. It is a round-the-clock work of twenty-four hours, for the most part. It is indeed comparable to the call to be a foreign missionary. The Gospel is to be lived and made known, if there are to be results. It requires great sacrifice and devoted service. The Lord did not say "go and play in my vineyard", but "go and labour in my vineyard". Any glamour that may enhance the call to be a missionary at the first, will soon give place to hard work, and the test of the spirit of endurance. Once the voyage is over, and the novelty of the new surroundings and strange people begins to fade away, life on the mission-field becomes earnest indeed. There are difficulties of language, long hours of duty, a trying climate, differences in temperament and innumerable things that demand much patience, perseverance and strength. The missionary is driven back in his need to Him who called and who alone is able to give the wisdom and the power to live and work in His name.

No work for God can ever be entirely easy, for before long in one way or another, we shall realise that there is an enemy who will try to work havoc wherever he finds an opportunity. Our Lord was spoken of as "the suffering Servant", but He has gone before and won the battle for us, and made the rough places smooth and the crooked places straight, if we have eyes to see. He does not ask from us the impossible for He gives us all things we need for the journey and the work He has appointed for us. He himself takes the heaviest end. He has himself fought the fight and drunk the bitterest cup, and trod "the winepress alone". "None of the ransomed ever knew." "How deep were the waters crossed, "Nor how dark was the night the Lord passed through, "Ere He found the sheep that was lost." But though he has done everything for us, he does not mean us to escape the trials that He allows to test our faith, and prove the reality of its existence, as well as to educate and strengthen it. It is helpful to recognise that the vocation of parenthood is not to be regarded as a lesser Call to service than that to other spheres of Christian work, and that it means much to God and His Heavenly Kingdom, and to mankind. The world is the better or the worse for every man and woman born into it - a fact that is generally overlooked. "No one lives to himself", and we well know how far-reaching for good or evil a single personality can be. For those who accept the training and the gift of a child as God's call and trust, there are great rewards, joys and compensations.

This can be especially the case for us as our children pass out of infancy and begin to walk and talk and increasingly make their awareness felt. These are the pre-school years and it is here that we have wonderful opportunities in helping to shape the mental outlook that does so much to form the character of the child. More than is generally realised they can be taught in these formative years in ways which will make life easier for the children later on. Some time ago a lady who had been unavoidably separated from her children in their early years, through having to live abroad, became very unhappy about them when they had reached their middle teenage years and later. In recounting her troubles to her friend, she said, "You had your children in their formative years, but I did not". Doubtless many of us look back with regret to those precious years and wonder if we made the best use of them. It has been said that the Roman Catholic Church claims that it can influence a child for life if it has the first six years to lay the foundation. In the present day the Communists do their utmost to capture the children body, soul and spirit, from the cradle, with their atheistic, anti-God doctrines, and thereby secure a nation. The heart and mind are well twisted through their ideology, and we know something of the dire results. This is quite apparent in many countries today. Would that the Christian nations and Christian parents exerted the same zeal in seeking to save their little ones for the only true Lord and Saviour of mankind.

The growth of a healthy child never stands still. A healthy child is a bundle of activity, fascinating and enterprising, as he seeks to express his thoughts and ideas, spending time on making raids of discovery the whole day long. As he lies asleep so peacefully and placid in his cot at the close of the day we wonder where all the energy comes from and are reminded of the charming little poem that comes from our cousins overseas.

> *You bad leetle boy, not much you care*
> *how busy you're keeping your poor Graun-pere,*
> *trying to stop you everyday chasing*
> *de hen round de hay,*
> *Why don't you geeve dem a chance to lay, leetle Batease?*
> *Off on the feil you follow de plough,*
> *den when you're tire you chase de cow,*
> *sicken de dog till they jump over de wall,*
> *so de milk ain't good for nothing at all,*

and you're only five and a half dis Fall, leetle Batease!
But leetle Batease, please don't forget,
We rader you're staying de small boy yet,
so chase de chickens and make dem scare
and do what you like to your old Graun-pere,
for when you're a beig feller, he won't be dere, leetle
Batease.

With energy come noticeable characteristics, likes and dislikes and innumerable indications of a character being shaped all on its own. Even in this early stage we can see that there is a need for gentle guidance and direction, if good habits are to be formed.

One of the earliest lessons every child should be taught is that of obedience. It was God's first lesson to our first parents. Obedience was to be the prime law by which fellowship with God and the supreme happiness of mankind were to be maintained, while disobedience meant the loss and the Fall of man. It was the first lesson and it is the last. Disobedience is rebellion against God and His laws. It is the root of all sin. It was not until our Lord came, and took upon himself our disobedience and took it away that he redeemed us. In our stead he was obedient to the Father at every step of his earthly life. He perfected the will of the Son of Man. He became obedient even unto the death on the Cross and thereby destroyed for ever the enmity caused by our disobedience to God. Without this obedience of Christ for us we could have no hope. He kept that which man failed to keep, and He did always "those things that pleased the Father". He took upon Himself the wrath of God against all disobedience and took it out of the way, nailing it to His Cross. "This", said God the Father, "is my Beloved Son in whom I am well pleased."

It was the disobedience, with which Samuel charged Saul, King of Israel, that destroyed him. One after another in the Old Testament disobeyed the heavenly vision and command, although the prophets constantly proclaimed that "to obey is better than sacrifice". In the New Testament our Lord persistently required obedience from His disciples. It was the great condition for all blessing. "Then are you my disciples if you keep my Word". "You are my friends if you do whatsoever I have commanded you." "If you love me, keep my commandments." And St Paul wrote, "For as by one man's disobedience many were made sinners, so by the obedience of One shall many be made righteous"; "the wrath of God comes upon the children of disobedience". Many Scriptures dwell on the same theme, and it is good for us all to search them out and "think on these things".

This lesson of obedience well learned is the secret of a happy Christian life, and it is no less the secret of a child's contented and happy life. It is far more important than many parents seem to regard it. It may not be too much to say that the root of most of the trouble met among teenagers lies here. One sometimes hears it said, "Oh, the child is too young to understand; when the time comes we will teach them then." Alas, that is generally too late. It is difficult to root out of a child the proneness to disobedience once it has begun to acquire the habit of doing as it pleases. According to a certain school of child training a child should never be suppressed. It should be allowed to follow its own inclinations and never be checked or hindered, or otherwise the child will have an accumulation of repressions in later years which will be harmful to its health in body and mind. Doubtless if the cause of such possibilities had been avoided in the first place there would have been no danger of suppression. This school of thought seems to be a re-bound from the old spartan days of our forefathers, and has gone to the extreme in the other direction with worse results than those traced back to our forefathers. It is in direct contradiction to all that God teaches us through His Word, and it can hardly arouse sympathy when in later years parents lament that their child has strayed far from the paths of right living. It is against all nature and God himself. Most folk will know of those who adopted that system. I think of one person and his wife who allowed their children "to do what they liked". The privilege was duly adopted by standing on the table just when desired, turning on the hot water taps, lying on the floor and screaming for long stretches of time, getting up in the night to play, climbing up the protesting neighbour's garden walls, etc. until everyone was miserable except the parents! One wonders were they really happy. No child comes into the world a perfect human being. All, even little children, are the children of the first Adam, with the same inclinations and the same seeds of death within them. The heart of a child is not different. Surely, then, there are good reasons why obedience should be taught and insisted on at a very early age. God expects it from every Christian parent. If we truly love the child and have its soul's salvation at heart, we shall certainly be on the alert to teach it God's first steps to Himself. A child can only learn about God in its earliest years through its parents. They are the mouthpiece for God. The child should see God through the life of its parents. None are so observant as the eyes of a child and its mind is easily impressed by what it sees. The whole horizon is filled with its parents whom it watches and looks for all day long. The mind of the young child is not filled with other things nor cluttered up with useless thoughts. It sees more clearly, thinks more purely, and considers more honestly and accurately than any adult. It will soon learn to read its parents like a book and will mark when they are in earnest or not. In fact, our actions speak louder than our words. Every time we make a promise and break it, every time we are tempted to tell an untruth, however well meaning it may appear, the child will register it in his mind, if only unconsciously. There are always plenty of opportunities throughout each day when obedience must be kept in view and practised. Most children will try to evade what to an extent they know ought to be done.

Every normal child is quick in the uptake and will soon assert his own personality, which is of course quite right. Nothing is more wearying to a child than the perpetual negative, "no" or "don't", and it is best to avoid it as much as possible. A small child can usually be led along the right way to do the right thing with a little effort on the part of the parent. As the child grows older a simple explanation can be made in such a way that it will appeal to him, though he should be led in the way of obedience from the start. If he wants to run the hot water tap down the sink he can be made to understand that the water has to be conserved and shared. Or, if he plays with fire, the dangers can be explained to him in a reasonable way. Much of what our Lord would have us like is bound up with the daily round of small things. If we train our child to consider others we shall be fulfilling His Law to love our neighbour as ourselves. Similarly if we persuade a child to refrain from trying to be the chief attraction in company, and that it is not right to interrupt when others are talking we shall be laying a foundation for the consideration of the other more than for the self.

It is a temptation to take the easier way and turn a blind eye when a child disobeys. It takes effort and patience to be always on the job. One is tempted to give it up and give in. Looking back on my own experience, I recall this difficulty. After having insisted that a certain thing should be done or not done, from time to time the thought came to let it go. But one soon realised the fatal mistake that was, for given an inch a child will take a mile, and most children will soon be quick to note the weakness of the parent and take advantage of it. If one insists on a line of obedience ninety-nine times and gives way on the hundredth the whole battle is lost. Of course one has to be careful not to insist on things that are unnecessary or unwise, and tact must be used. But patience will be rewarded, for after a time almost imperceptibly the child will have acquired the habit of obedience and be quite natural about it.

Obedience always makes a child happy, for he loves security and is conscious of it when he realises that someone stronger is holding the reigns of government. With obedience comes respect and, curious as it may seem, where there is obedience, there is also liberty. It reminds us of our own allegiance to the Lord. "If the Son shall make you free, you shall be free indeed." In Christ all things are ours, and we conclude that within His will we are indeed free, gloriously free. Fear is cast out, the future robbed of its threats, and we are delivered from bondage. St Paul calls it liberty, and so it is, but a liberty which can never be experienced but by Christ's bondmen. He has won it and purchased it with His own blood on the Cross, and it is His gift to us which He means us to enjoy. In Christ we have perfect security and all that goes with it, but we are warned not to abuse that which cost so much. In a similar way the child is free when it lives in an atmosphere of obedience. There will doubtless be clouds between it and its parents, but the sunshine of love will radiate its life. It is a rest to parents when they can trust their children and know that they will only do that which their parents wish. How helpful it is when the times of strain and emergency arrive and one has to trust the child. All will depend on how far obedience has been learned. Surely to a Christian parent the thought must come, "If my child does not obey me whom it sees, how will it ever obey God whom it does not see?" God has trusted us to use this holy service that we should be to our children as God is to us. "As I live by the Father, so you shall live by Me." And as we seek to live after the pattern prescribed for us, and do so before the child, so it is more likely that the child will follow in our steps. To shout, whip, or frighten a child into obedience is the wrong way, and far from God's way with us. His is ever a gentle, though sure, voice of strength and power. He would draw us to himself by love, patience, and all that is lovely. That is the better way with a child, but it takes time, self-discipline and thought, yet it pays every time, and tells greatly in the long run. Children should be taught to be courteous both to parents and to others. Some people think that courtesy is snobbery. On the other hand, many people who are not professing Christians are very courteous. It is a mark of Christian living which St Peter commended, "Be courteous", said the aged Apostle. Apparently by its context it should be the natural air of the Spirit-filled life, and so a little child can the more easily be taught this grace in its earliest years.

Many people consult their children at a far too early age. Children of two or three years old are asked if they would like to do this or that, to go here or there. That would be quite right a few years later but not at this stage. Much difficulty may be traced back to this fatal mistake. A young child cannot be expected to know what is best for him to choose, and it is putting power into his hands which he just does not know how to use. The serious thing about it is that he is being given the status of an adult while still a child, and in the effort to rise to the situation childhood is distorted and distressed. The growth and education of the mind of the child should be gradual, and vital lessons learned step by step. Maybe some people find it an easy way of getting round the requirement of obedience, but it can have very undesirable results. When so young a child is consulted and left to make a choice of his own, the chances are that it will start a whole course of difficulties that will continually crop up. He will soon realise that here is something that he can do just as he likes. He is likely to choose what his parents do not want him to choose and he knows it. But it has given him a power to act alone, and whether he chooses what he really likes will not be so important to him as the power of self-determination. This will of course have to come later on but in its proper time. If allowed now, he will go from the smaller things to the greater and develop a defiant attitude of mind. In this way, he will not be happy, but grow continually more discontented. He actually does not know what he really does want and certainly not what is good for him, and so he tries to make choice after choice which so unsettles his mind that he becomes utterly miserable and out of sorts with himself and everyone else. He throws in the sponge, as it were, and launches on a refractious course over most things to the distress of his indulgent parents!

A child in the first five years of his life should grow under wise control. It is right for the child and his or her own happiness and freedom to enjoy things that he is not responsible for and therefore not hampered with any form of restraint. It is also due to his home and surroundings, that he may learn at the best time of his life to live harmoniously. It is right for his teachers when the time comes to go to school and so that then the time (as in some cases) will not have to be devoted to taming a wild piece of humanity. There may be some who will disagree with this, but do we not all have to live within some measure of control? Is not a large amount of youth delinquency due to the distorted child-adult age we live in? It would appear that in most cases today the youth have never learned to obey or submit to parents from very early years. The long continuance of defiance and self-decision has woven itself into the warp and woof of their character, and life has become more difficult, indeed, not only for the individual himself, but for all concerned. Go where one will there must be a measure of law and regulation and order. To make a child develop into a good citizen his training must begin in the home and at an early age. Common sense brings home to us all the necessity of it. A motor car may have a smooth-going engine and all its parts may be in perfect order, but the one who drives must know the controls, and be able to use the car aright. All men and women should know how to order their lives in such a way, not only to avoid hurting others but to make the world a better place to live in. The astonishing thing is that many parents think their child should not be controlled in case it upsets him! He should be allowed to carve out his own character entirely unaided! The best of gardens must be weeded, the thorns and briars uprooted. Many of the vicious kind show comparatively little above ground for their roots run far beneath the surface, and are more difficult to deal with, but unless they are uprooted every gardener knows his garden will be a failure. So the earnest Christian parent will notice the undesirable things that crop up in the child's character and seek to eliminate them. Where obedience is made a major point in training a child, many other difficulties will automatically solve themselves.

The sin that accompanies disobedience is the telling of an untruth. Somehow they go together. Parents may have a horrible dread of their child becoming untruthful, yet gloss over the lack of obedience. Did not our first parents try to cover up their disobedience with a lie? It was the beginning of a long trail which extends down to us today. We all know the temptation to cover up some unfortunate act, if not with a deliberate untruth, at least with a compromise. When a child comes to accept obedience so that it becomes natural to him, a frankness and an affinity will grow between him and his parents. Conscience can and will work at a very early age and a wise parent will try to see to it that it is not abused or stained. It is not uncommon to find young folk who never hesitate to tell an untruth, and who seem to think there is nothing wrong in it and that it is just a case of acting expediently. Likewise it never occurs to them to think of obeying anyone or taking advice however well meant. Consequently they develop a self-centredness that in time produces an isolation which in turn makes life unhappy and purposeless. All kinds of subterfuges take place when lies and disobedience have gained a grip. It fills the juvenile courts, it spreads misery among the nations and breeds distrust the world over. Yet, where does it begin? In the tiny seed of a tiny heart, which all too easily many parents fail to detect until, having taken deep root downward it begins to bear fruit upward, and it has become hard to counteract. It is an important part of our call and our responsibility to God to see to it that disobedience and untruthfulness are overcome. God has made it all plain in His Word, if we have ears to hear and a heart to believe. Children are sometimes misled through hearing adult conversation, and the possibility is that they will pick up things wrongly, misunderstand and misinterpret them until their thoughts are filled with things that bring harm and dispeace. It is not always realised how much a child absorbs of what he hears and retains it in his mind even to having a nightmare in sleep! All undesirable discussion, newspaper articles, and adult stories are better kept out of a child's life, as they can easily breed fear and anxiety, as well as untruthful approaches to life.

"Blessed are the pure in heart for they shall see God" was a maxim that our Lord put forth - one that we should always make it our aim and that of our children to heed. "Train up a child in the way he should go, and when he is old he will not depart from it." These words may seem old fashioned today, but they seem to be effective. What a child has thoroughly learned in his early years will remain, if only in the remote crevices of the heart and mind or memory, and they will rise to the surface again in times of desperate need. A padre in the last war who went with the troops to the front related that in the last moments of a man dying on the battle-field, comfort came to him as he recalled some verse, hymn or prayer learned at his mother's knee or in Sunday School. All else seemed to be forgotten in that desperate moment, but the one thing that endures and outlives all else, the Word of God. Parents cannot measure the work they do while their children are young, if they teach and train them in the ways the Lord has commanded. "A child left to himself bringeth his mother shame", the wise man said in the book of Proverbs. For the sake of a child's welfare in its later years, the parent should be on the alert to hinder the growth of even apparently harmless things, which may eventually bring sorrow and pain to many. Disobedience is surely the arch enemy and not to be lightly treated or ignored. Life and death may at times depend on a child's instant obedience, especially in circumstances of danger as some have experienced. "I have no greater joy than to hear that my children walk in the truth", said the Aged Apostle John, which was surely an echo of the Word of the Lord concerning us and our children.

4

Pre-School Years

The simile of a shepherd and his sheep, used so much by God to enable us to understand heavenly things, is surely one of the loveliest and most appropriate. How stupid a flock of sheep can be! If one takes fright they all take fright, and fall into a panic, running here and there, tumbling over each other, none knowing the cause. What one does they all do. Their bland simple faces stare apprehensively at the stranger as he passes by. How foolish they seem, yet how attractive! The goats can climb the mountains and scale the rocks at will, seemingly able to take care of themselves, with no one being anxious about them. The sheep are different. They also wander off to considerable distances, or graze up the hillsides and in odd places, but they sometimes get lost or fall into the ditch, and get into difficulties of one sort or another. They need a shepherd. Every sheep farmer knows they need one to stride after the sheep and especially in winter to hunt for the lost ones who have gone too far or got buried in the snow. How often the shepherd has to lodge out all night with the sheep because he is unable to get them back into the fold.

So it is with us. We are all like sheep; "we have all gone astray". But the Chief Shepherd has made ample provision. How comforting to us all that He still says, "I am the Good Shepherd and give my life for the sheep." Yet, we are not just a flock of unidentifiable sheep, for we are told that "He calls his own sheep by name, and they hear His voice." They know when He calls them, and they follow Him. Are not the little lambs also precious in His sight? Yes, he carries them in His bosom, leads and keeps them from the perils of the way.

All Christian parents are His under-shepherds and are entrusted by the Chief Shepherd with the lambs - His lambs. Therefore the parents must be vigilant, too. We are reminded that there is such a thing as the wolf who seeks to destroy both sheep and lambs, scattering them as far away from the Shepherd as possible. No matter how much we may try to forget sin, and try to ignore it and turn our backs on its undesirable reality, nevertheless it is apt to dog our steps, subtly and invisibly no doubt, but showing itself in unexpected quarters - and little children are not immune.

One often hears the remark that a certain child has an irritable disposition, but it is very possible to overstate the case. Naturally as a child grows and moves around using its little feet and hands, it is bound to get into minor troubles and mischief. There will doubtless be real naughtiness at times which if we are wise we will be quick to check so that it does not recur. That will take courage perhaps, for as in the case of insisting on obedience the temptation will come to pass it over, or perhaps smile goodnaturedly at the child in the hope that he or she won't do it again. The likelihood, however, is that it will happen again. It is quite common to see a parent laugh and treat it as a joke which of course the child is quick to take advantage of. It can be seen almost everywhere, in buses, trains, restaurants, etc. Once when travelling by steamer out to the far East, two small children were on board. They were completely out of hand and climbed over all the ship becoming a nuisance to everyone, the captain included. He was rather a nervous man and took the care of his ship very seriously which was a heavy responsibility in itself. He was tormented at the sight of the children in perilous positions and lived in anticipation that he would have to stop the ship to search for children overboard. Those who have travelled have doubtless seen many such incidents, but strange as it may seem the children of Christians have often been regarded as the worst! Lightly passing over the first wrong, or treating children in an indulgent way will certainly lead to their getting out of control. Christians are apt to be more patient, hopeful, and gentle with their children, but neglect can soon work havoc. Some Christian parents seem to take so much for granted, and decide that everything will come right through prayer. If they are engaged in Christ's work and service they may conclude that God will take care of their children! But God expects us not only to pray, but to do all we can on our part, and especially to follow His teaching in regard to training the children He has given into our care. Misguided ideas along this line have led to many tragedies in after years.

Christian parents should be more sensitive to the issues that so easily arise. Our Lord ever drew attention to the smallest things of life; the sparrow, the mustard seed, the widow's mite, and the crumbs to be gathered that "nothing be lost". It is very necessary that we too are alive and quick to notice the so-called trivial things that spoil our children's life, so that we will be able to steer them from the pitfalls of later life. We recall how Eli grieved the Spirit of God over his sons. God brought judgment on him "because they had made themselves vile and he restrained them not". His love for his sons, or his fear of offending them, seemed to have been greater than his love for God. Is this not something of what our Lord meant when he said that those who follow Him are to love Him more than home, children or wife or brethren? He also said, "Thou shalt love the Lord with all thy heart, and with all thy soul, and with all thy mind, and with all thy strength". Not to restrain a child from doing wrong would seem to put love for the child before love for God. The ignoring of wrongdoing also does harm to the child, and allows evil teaching to get a strong hold of him. Real love both to God and to the child will not shrink from correction at the right time and place, and it will not count the cost of offending or being deflected by fear.

Of course some people do not recognise any tendency to wrong in a child. They think it rather "cute", and others think the child is too young and innocent to understand. Experience will show that the slightest misdeed is far better dealt with before it has time to get established. It is only too easy to tell a child right at the beginning of these things, than wait until repeated wrongdoing calls for sterner measures, and the child puts up a strong resistance when the parent attempts to correct him. Children can of course be provoking, but that is no reason for a parent to fly into a temper, and shout and scold and perhaps spank them. It is very easy for someone to vent his or her feelings in that way and to let off steam, but it does little good to the child. More than likely the child does not realise that he has done wrong. He may often have done it before and become used to it, and so is more concerned with his parent's anger than anything else. If he has been chastised he will be more concerned with his punishment than the reason for it. A small boy home from school one day was very upset. Obviously his feelings had been hurt. On inquiry it was learned that he had been punished by the teacher, but did not know why he had been punished. It was impossible therefore to advise him how to avoid being punished in the future. Later, it appeared that the teacher had been very angry and punished the whole class! No doubt it was the easiest way for her to express her resentment but it did harm and failed in its purpose.

For a parent to turn to corporal punishment frequently, as is often the case, is to cause the awareness or mind of the child to deteriorate. Such treatment appeals to the baser side of human nature and should never be resorted to except in extreme cases when all else has failed. It will bring out the worst side of a child. He will likely treat his playmates in the same way and it engenders a fighting and retaliatory spirit. A small child will sometimes attempt to hit his parents when told to do something he does not want to do. This kind of thing should be dealt with at once and never be allowed to happen a second time. It is the first appearance of a deadly weed and should be uprooted at once. If passed over and ignored, it will grow into a vicious habit and be more difficult to deal with, and will lay the foundation of many a heartbreak. It is more frequent in quite young children before they can talk much and explain themselves, so it has to be thoughtfully, though firmly, cured, and dealt with once for all. Some may say that a child has learned to defend itself, but that should only be when he has learned to control himself and have respect for others.

God lays the emphasis on chastisement rather than punishment, which is always meant to be corrective and constructive. He chastises all his children that they may be separated from the world and saved from condemnation. If we have gone astray, He will surely visit us, not for our destruction but rather for our salvation. All correction of children should be instructive and constructive, if we really want them to discern what is right and wrong, and to choose the right. Any other way is useless. Children can soon become hardened to punishment and scolding even to the point of ignoring it and going their own way, to the distress of their parents. Much can be avoided if the wrong is noticed and taken seriously at the very first. When corrective punishment has to be given it should definitely be done with a view to fixing the child's mind on the wrong done. A thoughtful parent can think up many ways of doing this. The main thing is to be determined that the child will know what it is punished for and to learn that he must never do it again. To make the child sensitive to what is right and wrong will save much sorrow later. An incident comes to mind about a small boy who, having nothing to do and doubtless finding time dragging a little, amused himself with a pin with which he scratched a long line across a new piano! It was of course rather an exasperating thing for him to do, but the most useful correction seemed to be that of explaining in a quiet deliberate way the sad state of affairs he had brought about, and then insisting that he stand and look at it until his sisters and brothers returned from school, which, however, was not very long. Such a thing never happened again.

God spoke on one occasion of having chastised His erring children by the Words of His mouth. It was also said that He will judge the nations by the sword of His mouth, which is the Word of God. Surely parents are meant to use words too. Care taken to explain the reason why something should be done or not done, put simply and plainly, is often all that is needed, and it is so much better than a hasty rebuke. A small boy and his cousin were recently playing in the garden of a friend's house, when unfortunately a ball went through a window. At once the boys went to the owner of the house and said, "We have broken a window in the garden and are very sorry. But it is right that we should come and tell you first, because the Bible tells us to do so." Could anyone do otherwise than forgive? Forgiveness should also follow confession at once. How quickly wrongs are healed and forgotten when there is readiness to acknowledge what has been done! Should we not train our children to do just that while they are still very young so that they will also know how to go to God with their needs and burdens without fear later on? How much sweeter would the world be if we were all quick to acknowledge when we have done wrong or injured another, instead of excusing ourselves and hiding things! How happy and peaceful our homes might be if our children are led to form this good habit of acknowledging faults and mistakes from an early age.

On occasion a child may be told that if he does a certain thing he will be punished. The child does it but the parent does not carry out the punishment, the result being that the child will not take his parent's word seriously and will in time mistrust his parent in other respects. It is important to carry out one's word whether in the nature of a punishment, a promise or reward. At all costs we should try to avoid the habit of continually threatening to do what we never carry out or even mean to. Many homes are quite unhappy because the parent is perpetually nagging at the children. It becomes such a habit that nothing else is ever expected. Surely it can best be avoided by tackling the difficulties at the very root at the beginning. Constant threatening and protesting, without insistence that right things should be done, and done at once, together with a wearying and nagging spirit, makes everyone in the home quite unhappy.

It is always wise to decide whether one is ready to carry out a punishment before the warning is given. Once given it should be carried out to the full. There are occasions when it would not be actually wrong and no harm would be done, when the parent should withhold punishment and deal with the problem in another way. It needs thought, tact and time to plan things in a right way and with the future in view. It is regrettable when parents often just cannot be bothered and so try to find an easy and quick way out whether it is for the good of the child or not, or when they adopt merely a temporary measure which is no more than a lazy or selfish way of evading an important duty. To follow that road will doubtless make life harder and increase difficulties and make one's own life miserable, and the home a place of discord. Would that we could all see how prompt action, the keeping of one's word, a little forethought and self-sacrifice, would make life happier for so many. Useless threats and hasty punishments soon harden any child, so that it will become unresponsive to a higher and nobler way of life.

Some parents seem to lack the moral courage to give their children the right corrective needed; or perhaps it is that they are afraid of falling into disfavor with their children, and resort to self-pity and whining, hoping thus to appeal to the child that way. But it seldom works. It is always fatal to allow a small child to be the master of the situation. Once he manages to do that, it may become a habit, when he will lose respect for his parents. Similarly if a school teacher for one reason or another loses the respect of his pupils, he will soon have his class in chaos and may as well give up, for the battle is lost. A child will respect those who are in authority over him, and who know well how to wield it wisely. Sometimes a mother breaks down in tears before her child, but it is a weakness that is to be deplored. It is false to suppose that it will make an appeal to the child's love and compassion. It may in some cases appear to succeed, but inwardly the child will love what it respects and can look up to, and that is something superior to himself especially in strength of character. In many cases where a child succeeds in reducing his mother to tears because of failure, he will be demoralised, and feel he has acquired a power which he can use to win his way, and a tyranny will take the place of respect.

Surely as Christians God commands our reverence above all else because He is above all and before all and He knows that love and adoration follow on the heels of reverence. With godly reverence comes joy, peace, security and confidence as well as love; God becomes the rock of our life and its strength. So with the child, parents must retain their superior position of respect, dignity and strength, if they are to keep the love of their children. Self-pity will never do that. If a child loses confidence and respect for its parents, it will likely turn elsewhere to what it can look up to and respect. In this connection also one has to be careful in one's statements and especially to be truthful in action and in word. We can only see through a glass darkly the spotless purity and righteousness of our Lord, but He does enable us through the Holy Spirit to see enough of what He expects us to do.

To retain the respect of our children has far-reaching effects and will do much in the years to come when they need advice and council at times of decision and crisis. Inconsistency on our part will weaken and have an ill effect on the minds of our children concerning our sincerity and integrity. In avoiding this pitfall of a child thinking he has got the better of his parent, it does not mean that the parent has got to shout or be severe in any way. A quiet voice can be powerful, and can often be most effective in the control of a child, humble him and make him sorry. It is a language that he will doubtless find different from that elsewhere, whether in the street, with his playmates, later in school and throughout life. The "still small voice" is most effective. But it is not a weak voice. A parent must be sure of himself when dealing with his child. He must maintain his stand in a dignified way, with firmness and be sure that he himself is right in the insistence of his demands. There is no quicker way of losing a child's respect than to punish him in the wrong way, for the wrong reason, in the wrong place and at the wrong time. Some people like to punish a child by rebuking him before his friends or other folk. That will most likely have an unhappy rebound. It is always unwise to punish one's child in public.

It is helpful also to avoid taking away a child's respect for himself. While not wanting to boost his ego, his parents should encourage him to behave in such a way as to make him realise he has the respect of others. To expose some fault or weakness by a foolish joke or rebuke, as some folk do, is liable to make him lose respect and confidence in himself. It will make him unhappy, and if persisted in, he will try to keep himself to himself and develop an isolated and autistic disposition. That is the kind of thing that distorts and destroys rather than corrects. It is better to talk to the child confidentially and in an encouraging way, while showing him the fault that should be overcome. It is necessary of course to avoid as much as possible making a child conscious of himself, especially when speaking of him to others in his presence. Some parents make the mistake of speaking about their child in such a way that he becomes very self-conscious and perhaps on that account will "show off". Our children are sweetest and most attractive when they are unconscious of themselves and quite natural. In a different way a child is sometimes spoken of in company about being difficult or peculiar in some respect. Before the rest of the family the mother may give a sigh, and look painfully at her child. This is certainly wrong. The child will in all probability ponder over the remarks of his mother and nurse them in his heart. It will play on his nerves, make him act strangely toward other children in the family, and may well make him feel lonely and isolated.

Whenever a child is a little different from the others, the parents should not show it or speak of it to others. The child should never feel that there is the slightest difference put between himself and the other children and should not suspect his parents of treating the others differently. To be unwise here can have serious effects on his health in body and mind. Many difficulties will die a natural death if wisely dealt with. Parents should make all their children feel equally cared for. It is easy sometimes to make a child a withdrawn or naughty where with proper treatment at the very start matters can be put right. Jealousy may try to spring up in a family but it should be quickly detected and overcome by the parents.

The business of correction will of course constantly come up in the early stages of the training of a child. A child should not be chastised because he won't eat his food. There is probably a reason for it which should be investigated carefully. It may be a digestive upset, which causes an aversion to certain foods, much as it may do with an adult. One certainly does not want to train a child to be difficult about food. The missing of a meal may help and can be in itself a kind of mental correction too. There may be psychological reasons for his behaviour, such as has just been mentioned when a child thinks he is different from the others and so ought to act differently or wants to attract attention to himself because he may imagine that he is neglected in comparison with the rest of the family. It is sometimes helpful to change the food frequently and make eating a fresh adventure. In any case it is better to find some other way rather than to resort to physical punishment.

Nothing hurts so much as wounded love. The parents who have won the love of their children and retain it have the best weapon for so-called punishment. Love begets love and the parents should love the child in the same unselfish way as God loves us. It is not a soft cuddly love like that given to a teddy bear that is hugged and then neglected for days on end after being thrown into a corner. It is a strong faithful love that the child needs a love that speaks louder than words. Occasionally our little ones may look miserable or pensive for no accountable reason. Even an adult passes through such moods. There are times when little children may feel lonely or perhaps fearful. Even a small babe has its fears especially when a strange hand lifts it up, carries or washes it. We all know how a baby will grasp tenaciously on to things through fear of falling. Fear attacks both small and great in some form, especially the more impressionable and sensitive. At such a time the child needs special comfort and to be made conscious of its parents' love. "Perfect love casts out fear". Love is always the cure for fear. It is a good thing when a child seems unhappy, for the mother to sit down and take the child on her lap and give herself to the child, chatting and showing a special interest in it, making the child feel that he is loved and needed. It is in that way that the fear is overcome and loneliness forgotten. I have seen such children, who were wanting to feel the touch of mother love, being misunderstood and being told "run away and play", "I am very busy just now". The child goes disconsolately away, but what an opportunity has been missed of laying a foundation for future confidence. How thankful we all are that God does not treat us in that way!

There are times when the heart is hungry for love to express itself, in spite of the many things that convince us that love is there. There are times when the longing to be assured of it comes again: so it is with the little child. Love is the best means for correcting, healing, and shaping little lives. Love is the greatest thing in the world and it is in our power to use it and wield it.

There are many avenues that open up daily in the training and upbringing of children through which the soul can be brought nearer to God, and the spiritual life can be taught and quickened. In the course of obedience and correction there are presented opportunities for revealing the parentage of the Heavenly Father's love, and in such a way that life-long impressions can be made, and godly habits formed, and noble characters moulded. Battles can be won in the earliest years which will prevent many a vale of tears bye and bye. Time is well spent when we are sufficiently at leisure with ourselves to show concern and interest in our little ones, by being attentive to their slightest desire for love, company and understanding. To join in their play, to romp and laugh, sing, in fact to become a child with our children at times, especially in the earliest years, will win their confidence in such a way that they will come to us continually to chat and talk things over when they are older. To give them freely of our time in those early stages is to secure their time when the younger years are over. How easy it is for a parent to lose out for ever by being selfish over time; by sending a child away to find occupation and company elsewhere because he or she "can't be bothered". The time may come when the grown child can't be bothered with the parent either. The opportunity was there once but it was neglected and it can never come again in the same way. Many a parent would give much to have the confidence of the child who once sought it in vain at the parent's knee.

Above all let us make time, then, to show our love to our children in a practical way, even in the course of correction, as our Lord does to us. How some of us look back and bless the Hand that chastised us sorely at times, when He permitted all His waves and billows to pass over our soul, and when He led us through storms that we might find Him for ever. Did it make us love Him less? No, it made us love Him ten thousand times more and we blessed Him for His providential planning and guiding, and for saving us from so much that, had we gone our own way, would have swept us for ever away from Him. His correction was the token of His Love and His personal Love to us, so that in all our affliction we knew He was with us and would bring us out into a "wealthy place".

Is it not also true with our children, as we correct them, wisely and kindly, and for their ultimate good in their relationship with God? The child thus trained will look back over the years and thank the parents who cared, and cared so much. He will forget much, perhaps, but the one thing that will remain and of which he will be most conscious is the love that wound its way into his heart and became lodged deep in the inner consciousness of his being.

5

The Place of God and His Word in the Home

"The Lord said, Shall I hide from Abraham that thing which I do? For I know him, that he will command his children and his household to do justice and judgment, that the Lord may bring upon Abraham that which He hath spoken." Later, through Moses God spoke and said, "These words shall be in thy heart, and thou shalt teach them diligently unto thy children, and shall talk of them in the way, when thou sittest in thy house, and when thou walkest in the way, and when thou liest down and when thou riseth up." In still later times, the Psalmist said, "Things which we have heard and known, we will not hide from our children, showing to the generation to come the praises of the Lord, and his strength, and the wonderful works that he has done, for He established a testimony, and appointed a law, which He commanded our fathers that they should make known to their children that the generation to come might know, even the children which should be born, who should rise and declare them to their children that they might set their hope in God." In the New Testament Jesus said to His disciples "Go ye therefore and make disciples of all nations, baptising them in the name of the Father and of the Son and of the Holy Spirit, teaching them to observe all things whatsoever I commanded you; and lo, I am with you alway, even unto the end of the world."

Here then is the parents' obligation to their children,

assured of the Lord's continual presence with them. Not only are we not to "hide" from them what our Lord has made known to us but we are to teach them "diligently". How thoroughly do the Holy Scriptures instruct the parents, and how detailed is the instruction given, to "talk" of God's Word when sitting in our house, or when walking in the way, lying down and rising up, night and day. It could hardly be more specific, but do we do it? It is rather odd that although parents know and can see how quickly a child grows and develops in mind and sense as well as in body, and how quickly he comes to discern the everyday things of life, yet in the matter of the Christian Faith, any such teaching is largely omitted, because, "the child is too young" and "later will be soon enough". But that surely is not what God expects from us. The mind of the child is naturally more receptive and open to God than that of most adults. As a rule he will accept the fact of God quite simply if led that way right from the first. One cannot but feel that this omission on the part of the parents, or perhaps it may be reluctance, arises from the fact that the Christian Faith to them is a religion only and something apart from everyday life. It must be kept in a compartment of its own for special occasions. I have seen it treated in that way, and as the children grew older small doses of this religion were, as it were, doled out, like a dose of castor oil! Is it to be wondered at that when the children are old enough they will have nothing to do with the religion of such parents, to the latter's dismay?

But the Christian faith is quite different from a cold form of professed religion. Our faith is to be as natural as our physical life. We are to talk about it in all places and circumstances, to mingle it with all we do and plan and to take for granted the spiritual Life we own and profess as part of our early life. It should be the spice of life, the joy that none can take away, and the Song of Songs in our heart. A very happy memory comes to my own mind when taking country walks with children. Our conversation would turn on to spiritual things and the Word of God in quite a natural way. On at least one occasion our discussions went quite far into the meaning of the Christian walk as we wandered our way through the pathways of the lovely hilly countryside and it seemed as though we were reaching after things beyond the ability of some to follow, and it was suggested that we change the conversation from those deep things of God. But immediately the young voices said, "Oh do go on, we understand and we do want to know about it." It seems so easy to "talk" about the things of God when "we are in the way", quite naturally and freely, and God seems to draw near opening up the understanding and making Himself known and felt to the young hearts reaching out after Him. God surely means us who are parents to make the knowledge of Him and His Word natural in every way, and to apply it to our daily affairs so that the young child becomes familiar with God's way of life at a very early age. We can talk about the characters in the Bible and discuss why some succeeded and some failed, how they came to go astray, and why God was displeased, and on the other hand how the heart of God rejoices when he finds those after His own heart whom He can trust to reveal His Word and plan for our salvation. The Bible is full of matter for such conversations in all ages. The important thing is that we bring God into the atmosphere of the home, to share all our joys as well as our tears. The aim should be to win our children for God by helping them to realise and feel He is with them and knows all their interests as He also desires them to know Him and share their life with Him. We need to make children feel perfectly at home with Him and never allow them to regard God in an austere way. Some years ago when addressing a mothers' meeting, before it was time to speak, one of the Church elders said a pungent thing or two to the women, among which was the remark "Don't make the father a bogey in the home by saying, when the child has done wrong, `I shall tell your father', or `wait until your father comes home and he will punish you'. Remember the father has been away all day and he does not want to come home to that kind of thing." How true it was the women seemed to know well. Yet is this not just the way parents represent God to their children? "Someone is watching and will be angry"; "God will punish you for being naughty", and other threats may be made. What an awful conception can be given of God our loving Heavenly Father to the mind of a child! We read what Job's friends' great mistake was: "My wrath is kindled against you, for you have not spoken of me the thing that is right". God is, apparently, very sensitive as to what we say about Him, and how we represent Him to our children. We are to teach our children that our Heavenly Father is One who loves them above all else, who knows them and understands them above all others. That He is their best Friend to whom they can go with everything and tell Him, and that there is no need to hide anything from Him, for He loves to hear everything and also to hear them say, when they have been naughty, how it came about and how sorry they are. It is this helping of a child to be perfectly frank with God in his young years that will help him all through his life. How lovely it is when a young child accepts God as part of his daily life, and when he walks and talks, goes to bed and gets up. Children soon make habits and they will soon acquire the habit of counting on God if they are taught aright. "Except you become", our Lord said, "as one of these little children, you cannot enter the Kingdom of Heaven". Did the little one believe whom Jesus called to Him? Of course he did. God is love and the child is taught to love Him without fear or dread in his very early years, and will most likely retain in his inner soul the Love that never fades and the blessedness of the Companion of his childhood.

But some may ask, "How can this come about?" Much depends on the parents' personal attitude the firm resolve of love and faith, as soon as the child is born and indeed before, to bring up the child in the conscious love of God who gave them the child for this end. Continual prayer is a necessity and will help to focus the attention continually in the right ways. We have to lift up our hearts without ceasing for our children. We can pray over them as they lie in their cots, and form the habit of prayer as we put them to bed and on various other occasions. As this is done constantly the child will become aware of it and the Holy Spirit will interpret and convey the sense of the Presence of God to him. We so often forget that our God is more anxious and concerned for the spiritual welfare of our children than we can ever be, and also that the Holy Spirit is unceasingly at work as we try to do our part. We may imagine that it all rests with us, but the Power of God is at work alongside of us and it is a case of our working together with Him. It lies with us to bring about the atmosphere in which God can work.

This natural atmosphere of God in the home can be greatly hindered by the disunity of the parents in spiritual things. It is not unusual to find that while both parents truly believe and love the Lord, attend Church and engage in devotional meetings, yet they cannot talk freely to each other about the Word of God, neither can they kneel in prayer together when alone. Somehow there exist barriers between them, channels are blocked so that the natural flow of the mind in spiritual things does not take place. This will hinder the growth of spiritual aptitude in the child. Christian parents should face up to this problem. It can be overcome and every effort should be made to do so. There are likely reasons for the trouble. It may be that one parent feels that he does not "live up" to things as he ought to and fears the criticism and condemnation of the other. It is helpful to remember that none of us can claim any righteousness of our own, that we are all unprofitable servants in God's sight, and that all are guilty before Him; and so we should resist the temptation of comparing ourselves one with the other so as to avoid all criticism of each other. As our eyes are ever upward toward Him we shall cease to consider ourselves, knowing that He knows us better than we know ourselves and that He loves us in spite of all and desires that we should come before Him with all our infirmities, for only as we do come can they ever be overcome, and all obstacles will melt away before Him. Prayer together does wonders. It changes things. In place of harbouring prejudices we become more mindful of the Lord and less self-conscious before each other. I have known how this fear between parents can harm the atmosphere in the home; as we love the Lord it should be mastered. Few things are more desirable than to see husband and wife on their knees before the Lord. They will rise up different, and there will be a bond of union between them through which the Holy Spirit can work effectively.

Another hindrance to the right atmosphere in the home is the lack of definite assurance of salvation in the faith of one or both parents, misgivings about the Word of God and the lack of a personal knowledge of God. In these hurried days so many people seem just to drift along, professing to be Christians, going to Church and religious meetings and perhaps taking part in church activities, and yet have never faced up to the definite and direct challenge of the Lord to them personally. They have never had an encounter with Him and found Him to be their only Captain and the ultimate Authority of their life, and the only way to victorious Christian living. This fact came unexpectedly to the fore during the "Tell Scotland" Campaign with Dr. Billy Graham. Many came to the council rooms, because they had come to realise that they did not quite know where they stood. They had never made any clear decision and had no assurance of forgiveness of sins in their hearts. Good earnest people were among those who came forward who had been very faithful in their church adherence and yet were strangely perturbed. Every soul needs to be sure of its anchorage, and where this is uncertain the home is liable to be unstable and it will have its reaction on the children. We cannot lead our children where we have never been ourselves. We cannot give them what we have never had ourselves. We cannot help them to build upon the Rock if we are not sure that we are resting on it ourselves.Whatever the reasons or hindrances that make for disunity in the home, a united effort must be made to overcome them, so that the children may be given every opportunity to know God, and so that prayer for them may not be hindered. It is very plainly pointed out in the Holy Scriptures that God expects much from the home. It is the cradle for heaven, the Bethany where Jesus loves to tarry and where the Word of God is freely discussed and talked about. Things spiritual and eternal should be commonplace and mingle with every hope and purpose, and especially where parents and children bow their heads before God or kneel together and declare their allegiance to him as well as commit all things into His hands and ask for the daily supply for every need. In this intimate and personal way the parents make known that they are inheritors together of the grace and glory of God and that it is quite as natural to converse with God as to partake of our food round the table. It is sad to see how few homes maintain the habit of "saying grace" before meals, at all times. It is a wonderful opportunity for the parents to foster the spirit of gratitude in the hearts of their children. Ingratitude is a bitter herb to have in God's garden. Our Lord was conscious of it when He said to the leper who returned to give thanks, "But where are the nine that are not found to give glory to God?" In giving thanks for the material bread we can lead our children to seek and give thanks for the heavenly Bread without which they cannot grow and be sustained. The pre-school years of our children are the special prerogative of the parents, through which they have the most important opportunity to lay the foundation of a healthy and strong life, materially, morally and spiritually. They are the precious years that belong to them and through which much can be done to temper and shape those that follow on. These are the years that so many pass over too lightly, only to realise later on that ground has been lost which cannot be recovered. They are the impressionable and character-moulding years before the mind is crowded with other things, and the children pass on to come under the influences outside the home, whether at school, business, or university, and in the wide world beyond. A child's heart is a seed-bed, either for good or for evil. The words "Bring up a child in the way he should go and when he is old he will not depart from it" may seem old-fashioned, but the principle still holds good. Many things take root right at the start of life, when truthfulness and faithfulness in everything are of great importance. Parents are ambassadors of God to the child and as such represent God to the child, so that their exhibition of integrity and rightness should fill the horizon of the child's mind. He will naturally see God through his parents, for it is all he has to go on. As our Lord declared the Father, so He expects us to declare Him especially to our children. We are God's interpreters so that in all the avenues of daily living we are to make him known in truth and righteousness. Only so will they come to put their trust in Him because they have so learned through us that "He is faithful who promised". Young children are soon sensitive to right and wrong and fair judgment, and one has always to be alert over these issues. Quite thoughtlessly a parent may condone one child and condemn another for much the same thing, or be more favourable to one and rather prejudiced against another, even quite unintentionally. But a sensitive child will quickly take notice, and silently nurse his grievance. Absolute fairness to all children in a family, with complete equality of treatment, is essential for the happiness of a family. Naturally some children attract more than others, and seem more lovable. Yet, how often this has given rise to jealousy, bitterness, resentment and stubbornness in the child who appears to be less attractive. Unhappily this has rankled more or less throughout the lives of some people. Most of us have met those who have suffered in this way. Probably the parents were unconscious of what was taking place, and blind to any harm that they may have done. Children vary much in a family, and sometimes one may seem dull and unattractive, but when he becomes conscious of it he may well shut himself off from the company of the others, always standing back and letting the more attractive child do all the talking. Yet, in later years what seemed so slow and dormant in earlier years, may blossom out into a sterling character, a reliable and comforting personality. We are eternally grateful to our heavenly Father that He never discriminates between His children. He loves them one and all equally. The sheep which strays on the mountainside, the prodigal who wastes his life among sinners, the blind, the dumb, the simple, God loves them all to the uttermost, the unlovely and the loveable. Would that we as earthly parents could be filled with this amazing impartial love for each and all our children, so that we could be sensitive to all their needs in learning and growing up. The upbringing of children is also a re-education of ourselves.

We soon discover many faults in ourselves as we seek to steer the little ones along the right road. We notice things that we would not have been aware of but for the child. Sometimes a child will make a request to his mother and then when it has been turned down address the same request to his father but in such cases both parents must stand together. Even if both parents are not agreed about something, yet for the sake of the child they must be united at such junctures, else chaos will prevail in the home. There should never be any appeal allowed from one parent to another, neither should any criticism of one to the other be tolerated. United the parents must stand together if they are to win through. Unselfishness is one of those things that a child should be taught as early as possible. "Thou shalt love thy neighbour as thyself" was to fulfil "the Royal Law", as the Apostle James said, the law that should actuate all our motives throughout life. Great emphasis is laid on it all through the Scriptures. Our Lord reiterated it, and the ancient Apostle John seemed to have in his last days as his one theme the love of God and the love of one another. "By this shall all men know that you are my disciples, if you love one another", was among the parting words of the Lord Jesus to His disciples. Love is ever unselfish and it is among the most precious things we can teach our children diligently. Human nature left to itself is selfish and destructive, and these traits can soon be seen in most children. We can begin by teaching a child that most things are given to share with others, and not for himself alone, and generally a child will enjoy sharing things once it is induced to do so. Sharing breeds companionship and friendship, and will encourage thoughtfulness for others as well as love and fellowship.

Children do not naturally like loneliness, and to get away from it they will often, of their own will, try to share what they have in order to make friends with other children. It is a spiritual instinct. God does not mean us to live alone, for He understands human nature, and meets our need. He not only loves us individually but enlarges our capacity for love, and commands us to share our love if we would be loved by Him. Instinctively this will be received by a little child and with practice become second nature to him.

But there are other forms of unselfishness that a child can be taught. A child may insist on being first in most things, and as he grows older he may like to monopolise the attention of his parents, and try to keep them occupied with him, or distracted when they are engaged in some special duty or when they are holding a conversation with some friends they are entertaining. A friend in need of help, advice or spiritual fellowship may call, but goes away dispirited because a child was determined to keep his parent occupied with him. In many such little ways, often too insignificant for the parent to notice, selfishness can be allowed to persist and spoil a child. A quiet talk and explanation in a very simple way will often work wonderfully, or if the child is too small other ways can be used to help him to be unselfish.

As children grow older, if not taught earlier, they may, to the embarrassment of others, be allowed to interrupt and even dominate the conversation and discussion of adults, until they succeed in mastering the situation. How frequently one hears, "Oh, those children"! Children are not kept in their playrooms as often as they used to be, but are allowed to listen to conversation far above them and not good for them to overhear, and which may indeed be rather damaging to their minds. Children continue to be more contented for a longer time, if they are kept occupied with their own play things and away from the harrowing remarks of adults. In any case children need to be taught to listen to the injunctions and to respect others, and in that way they will begin to learn something in the way of unselfishness and self-control, if only unconsciously. Children sometimes seem to take a delight in destruction. They may feel suppressed over something withheld from them and find an outlet in kicking or abusing or damaging things around them. Some people think that it does not matter how children pull things to pieces, scratch or tear and generally misuse things whether their own or other peoples'! One is amazed sometimes at the way people allow their children to be destructive, and a nuisance wherever they go. Surely an important lesson for every Christian parent is to teach his children that we are sent into the world to use it but not to abuse it, to make the best of things and especially to honour and respect the property of others. Disregard for others' interests and the "couldn't care less" mentality lie at the root of much misery and pain in our world today. The Scriptures remind us that we have a duty to our neighbour to care for his property as our own and his feelings too. These things can be taught to a child through the things he handles and sees every day. It may be the way of human nature in its depravity to destroy and pull down, but most children can be taught otherwise with a little ingenuity and patience. It is easy for children to think that the world is made for them, but the sooner they learn to realise how to fit in to it and take their place in it the happier and more contented they will be, and so will their parents! A child can be very pliable in skilful hands and once taught he will settle down and be contented, a joy to himself and everyone else.

We must certainly dwell on the practical ways of teaching the child, but there is another side to it all. One of the most delightful ways of training the mind is of telling our children stories or of reading to them. Through this means the mind can be directed into right channels of thought, right ambitions, and a right estimate of things. The stories of the Bible translated by the parent into everyday language and made vivid and living can prove particularly helpful, especially if the parent perseveres with them. Good stories at bedtime lay up good treasure in little hearts. Little incidents that occur in the daytime can be likened to something previously read and the true way reinforced in a natural way. I remember a Christian mother who made a point of telling Bible stories to her little boys asking one evening, "What story shall we have tonight?" At once the answer came, "Tell us about Joseph, that is the best story in the world". Of course it was, for it was a family story especially for boys, brothers, a loving father and a true story of forgiving love, with a "happy ever after". It is indeed a story that supplies plenty of ideas of how to live in the best way and how to avoid the worst.

It is always rewarding to store a child's mind with the Holy Scriptures. It is like storing up ammunition for the day of battle, or storing up food for drought. It is helpful to the child to teach him to memorise verses, passages, and stories from the Scriptures, so that the Word of God becomes familiar to his mind. Memorising what is learned in that way in these early years will remain in the memory. It prepares the way for the Holy Spirit to work in the heart and mind. It is providing our children with the armour which they will stand in need of from time to time on life's journey. At one time a missionary family were travelling down a long dangerous river in a foreign land. After a long and trying day the captain failed to make the usual safe harbour at sunset, and the boat was forced to anchor in unsafe quarters for the night. In the brief twilight the father walked along the beach with his eldest son, a small boy. It was an eerie place and infested with robbers, and the child seemed to sense the danger. Looking up into his father's face he said, "Daddy, doesn't it say somewhere in the Bible,'What time I am afraid I will trust in the Lord'"? "Yes", said the father, "it is in the fifty-sixth Psalm", and the child was comforted by the sense that God was nearer than any danger. That verse had been learned previously and in the moment of need the Holy Spirit revived it in his memory and made the words speak personally to the heart of the child, and as always the Word of God brings strength and power. Many such incidents could be related. But can there be a better way for the child than for the Word of God to be stored in the mind of the child? Like the Apostle Peter we might say, "Silver and gold have I none, but such as I have I give unto you" - unto you our children. God does not speak "out of the blue", but He speaks with no uncertainty the Living Word through the written Word. That Word is His provision for all we need throughout life. Should we not then provide our children with such a sure Companion who never forsakes them, a Guide who will never mislead them, a Friend who will never fail them, and a Comforter who will be with them at all times, in all places, in sunshine and storm, even to their old age?

    It is the parents' great opportunity in the pre-school days especially, to store the minds of their children with the written Word of God, that they may have the best equipment for all time. Of course they will not understand much at the time, but as they grow older and move away from home and into their life's work, it will go with them, and God will not fail on his part to make good use of the seed that the parents have sown into their hearts, which is the Word of God. By prayer it "will accomplish the thing whereunto it is sent". This is the thing that God has commanded us to do, "to teach His Word diligently", "to talk" our children into the knowledge of God and to do the will of God in His Kingdom. These are the golden hours and God forbid that we should miss them. It does not mean that the life of a child should be dull and uninteresting. Taught in the right way there is life, joy and sunshine in God's Word for a child. Plenty of play and activity mingled with right instruction in an unpresuming way often inform the happiest years both of child and parent. Recently a young man, now experienced in the ministry of the church, who was conscripted during the war and served in India, mixing with all types of men, said to his mother, "We had a very happy childhood". It was said quite unexpectedly during a conversation, and what greater joy could a mother have? That young man was taught in his childhood along the lines advocated in these pages. A child naturally lives in a little kingdom of his own and he will carry through life chiefly those things which make the memory fragrant. All nature is alluring to a child. The trees, flowers, birds, and the changing skies, the rain and the dew drops, can all be turned into parables of heavenly things, windows through which a child can see God and know Him and love Him, as Creator and Saviour. As the Psalmist says, "Day unto day utters speech and night unto night shows knowledge; there is no speech nor language where their voice is not heard." And St Paul says, "There are, it may be, so many kinds of voices in the world and none of them is without signification". The world around us teems with reminders of God's activities, and they are His witnesses for those who have eyes to see and ears to hear.

It is a refreshing thing both for parent and child to search out together the treasures that God scatters around us. The changing seasons, each with its purpose, the stars and the wonder of the Milky Way, the little creatures of earth like the tadpoles, the moths and the butterflies, the croaking frogs around the shining pools, the ways of the hare and of the fox, all of them have their lessons and fascination. The tiny animals who store for the winter, the cuckoo who makes others do its work, the common robin and the blackbird in the garden, the rolling tides and the myriad particles of sand, all teem with lessons God is teaching. How much better it is to fill the minds of children with these things, rather than with the artificial things that the world produces for the young people today! Nature can supply a child with an abundant interest, which will become a living reality. "Whatsoever things are lovely, think on these things."

There are many useful and attractive books, and children for the most part love the book world. Naturally the parent has to be careful to choose the right kind of literature for the child to read. How much good can be done by good books, yet how much harm can also be done by books that are far from being good! As a rule children love to be read to. Biographies, histories, adventure and travel stories - and missionary lives for Sundays! - are rich in information and wisdom for the child. For the young child the parent can interpret, explain and simplify much of what is read. Some of my own happiest memories are of the times when to a little audience we read some of the life stories of the world of nature. We discussed what we read and learned together, the children all the time increasing in knowledge and storing their minds with many possibilities. Children are ever fond of asking questions which at times can be rather trying, but it is the way they begin to think as they learn, and it is important that right questions should be asked and true answers should be given. It is unwise to evade the truth, even if the truth is unsavoury. There is always a way by which the sincere Christian can guide the thought of a child through truth to the Lord who makes all things work together for good to those who love Him.

An aged saint in America once wrote to the writer, "All your children shall be taught of the Lord". What an encouraging promise to relay from the Lord! God's promises often seem paradoxical. He tells us what He will do, and at the same time tells us also what to do. His promises beget promises and our efforts can only succeed within the fulfillment of His will. If we do teach our children diligently, as He commands, God will also surely fulfil His promise by teaching them Himself as well. It is something we all need to ponder, why God commands us to do what only He can and will make effective. He commands us according to His will and at the same time wills what He commands. There is also a warning here: to be faithful and true to all that He reveals. Our teaching ability may be very poor and feeble; we stumble and make many mistakes and sometimes have a deep sense of failure. It is like a child who strives to write his first letter. The letters are crooked, disconnected, uneven and sometimes unrecognisable, but the parent or teacher comes to the rescue by placing a steady, firm hand over the child's weak effort and so the letter is written and the child is happy. So our glorious Lord knows all too well how often we try and seem to fail, and how tempted we are to be discouraged. How comforting to realise that He has the heart of the truest Parent, for He is our Heavenly Father and knows all our failings and shortcomings, but with His strong and skilful hand, He will make perfect that which we do so imperfectly.

6

First Years at School - Readjustment

"As an eagle stirs up her nest, flutters over her young, spreads abroad her wings, takes them, bears them on her wings, so the Lord did lead them." "He kept them as the apple of his eye." The day must come when the young eaglets are getting too big for the nest. They have been fed and reared, but they have also grown. They have been preparing for their mission in life and must go forth. They can no longer be satisfied through the unceasing work of the mother bird. They are on the wing themselves and must soon be put to trial. The mother eagle, taught of the Lord, stirs up her nest and gets things going. However much she would like to continue hovering over her young and keep them there, she knows it is quite impossible. She spreads out her wings and she topples them out of the nest, though not out of her care, for as they flutter downwards, she swoops beneath them and bears them upward again on her broad strong wings. Again and again she carries them aloft, ever persevering until the eaglets' wings come into action, and the tiny wings spread ever broader, becoming stronger and are at home in the elements until finally they soar aloft on their own and do battle with the wind and storm in search of food and sustenance. It is a graphic picture of the way God led His people out of Egypt "through the waste howling wilderness", as Moses called it, ever bearing His people up again and again, as they sank in disobedience and rebellion. But he taught them to journey on, forgiving them over and over again, raising them up to Himself until their ears were attuned to hear His voice and their hearts were ready to obey Him, and He could make of them a great nation and His chosen people for ever.

The time comes when our little ones begin to leave their nest in the home. The growth of mind and body necessitate it. The energies of the growing child demand it. The heart of the mother often clings round her little lambs who have sheltered under her care hitherto, and with some anxiety she thinks of the cold blasts and the rough winds that may swirl around them as they launch out into life, even though the start may be a very gentle one. The lambs will grow and the skipping days, all too short, slip away. Yet would we wish it otherwise? The babe in the cot must outgrow its narrow quarters; the child must learn to walk and talk, and so the time to start school arrives. We know also that in our Christian life we do not remain where we once were. We once feared that the joy of that ecstatic hour would vanish away when we first found our Lord and Saviour or rather when He found us; the days were heaven on earth. But the Lord says to one, "Go call Peter", and to Philip, "Find Nathaniel", and to Mary Magdalene, "Go and tell my brethren". How much there was to learn and to be learned! The testings, trials, and storms all had to be part of our training, if we were to be steadfast and unshaken in the faith. As we grow older and look back over the years we know that God had a purpose in all the discipline of life and the hard things that we had to endure; "the stormy wind fulfilling his Word", as the Psalmist says. "Thou canst not see my face and live", said the Lord to Moses, "but thou shall see my back parts." So it is as we look back, and however much it had cost would we have had it otherwise? As the poet Cowper said,

> *His purpose will ripen fast,*
> *unfolding every hour,*
> *the bud may have a bitter taste,*
> *but sweet will be the flower.*

Parents have mixed feeling about this intrusion into their nest when the time arrives for the children to go to school - that is particularly the case with the mother. Some people, evidently, are only too glad when school time arrives. They may have a busy life and are glad to have the child taken care of for a few hours each day. But children come to the stage when they need more occupation mentally as well as physically. To the earnest Christian parent it brings some apprehension. Hitherto the control of their child has been entirely in their own hands. He has been loved, nourished and cared for in body and mind, as well as sheltered from much that will likely come his way now. Other influences will be brought to bear upon the child's life, and the mother wonders if her children will be all that she would choose and desire. Then there is the mixing with other children from a variety of homes. Will lessons taught be unlearned? In any case new phases in the pattern of living will be followed, and the anxious parent cannot but have some anxiety over whether her child will be different.

It is wise, however, to face the new situation by accepting the facts and doing all she can to make things go well for the child, just as the mother eagle does for her young. If she has availed herself of the first years in fitting and preparing the child according to the pattern God has indicated to us, then things are likely to go well. Good seed will now begin to bear good fruit. If the child has learned to obey, to be considerate of others, been taught to listen and has been trained in good habits, then school should be a happy place from the start and the child will be spared from having to learn much in what may well be a less congenial and more difficult way. Some children are sent to school by parents who could not control them at home. School can then become a kind of escape for the easy-going parent. The harassed teacher may have a hard task in bringing about what should have been done in the home. How easily a good class of children is spoilt by a few difficult ones, which need not have happened if the parents had spent more time in preparing their children in the right way. Many sad stories could be related about undisciplined children, not least some of those who have been sent to Boarding Schools! Unfortunately in these cases school has sometimes left a bad impression on the child's mind for years, which should not have happened.

If Christian parents have been considerate in the training of their children and have won their confidence, then their relations with them will be able to continue along much the same line as in the earlier years - at least for a considerable time. It must be recognised that they have gone to school for a purpose and that this is the beginning of that part of their training that is to prepare them for their ultimate vocation in life. It is wise to take a long view of things even now and determine to make the best of all the opportunities that come along, and to put aside all preconceptions and prejudices. The child may be a little hesitant at first over the school adventure. The thought of being separated from the parent may bother some and they will need to be encouraged and be disarmed of their fears, but with help there is no reason why the child should not soon adapt himself to the new life. New occupations will certainly make their own appeal to him.

The important thing is that the parent should be deeply interested in the school life of the child. Once the child realises this, his confidence and feeling of security in school life will grow and his interest in everything will be intensified. Children do not like to feel they are being got rid of, or that they are not wanted. Through the right attitude of the parents, the child will look forward to telling the parents what happens at school each day. He or she will naturally want to share these with those he or she feels love them. Parents ought to do all they can to encourage this, by taking a keen interest in all that concerns the child. It is in this simple way that new relations become established between child and parent which in its very small way is the beginning of what will later prove an avenue of good influence for right decisions at a critical time. If children feel free to talk over with their parents their school life, their friends and games, and all that pertains to their new life, they will be happy and school and home will be bound together in a meaningful and helpful way. Unfortunately

First Years at School—Readjustment

some parents do not have much patience in these matters, and even show impatience which discourages the child from opening up his mind and airing his thoughts about his school activities. But they will lose much if they do not try to retain the confidence and frankness of earlier years. The outcome may be that the child will quite unconsciously develop an independent personality too soon, and begin to hold back things from his parents that the latter ought to know or be aware of. Moreover the opportunity is then missed for emphasizing the good that is being taught at school, and of smoothing out difficulties. This beginning of school life marks a big change from the simpler early years in the shelter of the home, although of course the child's early impressions continue to have their due effect. A new world is opening up, for good and possibly also for things not so good. In a miniature way school life is already life in the world, and through school the impact of the world outside will increasingly be felt. At school the child begins to mix with other children who come from different backgrounds and with different training, and who naturally have a variety of dispositions and characteristics. The beginnings of many new experiences are here and the parents who desire the well-being of their children will want to become involved in the child's school affairs from the very start. These first six years of school life lay the foundation for another six, the earlier preparing the child in mentality and general outlook for the latter, in none of which can the parents afford simply to leave everything to the influence of others. These are crucial years that do much to form the more difficult teenage years, when parents will have to adapt themselves to their children. Too many parents treat these early school years as insignificant. One mother was recently heard to remark "Eleven years old is early enough to begin to teach a child". Another mother quickly answered, "Eleven years may be too late - you cannot really teach them much then." This conversation was among parents at a young women's gathering. In these days when children seem to mature earlier than they used to, when they hear so much about adult affairs through the radio and television, parents need to be on their tiptoes, if they hope to guide their children into a right way of life and thought. It is never too early to begin. The fostering of spiritual life in children must also go on, and the impression made on the child of the claims of God through outward and visible things is the special responsibility of the parents. This character-formation is like a building. Even though the foundations may be good, the building itself must not be flimsy and faulty.

It may seem rather out-moded to refer to the Ten Commandments. "Oh, we never think of them now", someone says. Nevertheless they are still the basis of all our civilisation. Our laws for the welfare of the state spring from them, and they remain the foundation of all clean and honest relations between peoples and nations. The principles set out in the commandments should permeate the atmosphere of every home, and be built into people's characters. Some may argue that the Law has been superseded by Grace. Grace and the Gospel are the fulfilment of the Law which has taken place through Christ. But the spirit of truth and righteousness in the Law can never be superseded and have indeed been finally embodied in the Lord Jesus, who summed up the whole Law in the golden rule: "Thou shalt love the Lord thy God, with all thy heart and with all thy soul and with all thy mind, and thy neighbour as thyself." Jesus in fact enlarged the Commandments in the Beatitudes and the Sermon on the Mount. Here we have plain instruction in the way that we should train our children, for which school days afford plenty of opportunity.

Parents who are anxious that their children should grow up in the fear of the Lord are concerned over the modern trend to depart from at least two of the Commandments: "Remember the Sabbath Day to keep it holy" is the first, and the other, "Honour thy father and thy mother that thy days may be long in the land which the Lord thy God giveth thee." The difficulty over these injunctions grows more acute as the children grow older and mix with so many others who come from less God-fearing homes. As a nation and people we seem to be ever departing from the old conception of the Sabbath Day. The love of pleasure and leisure has invaded our land, and finds its expression in Sunday sports,

First Years at School—Readjustment

picnics, and special bus tours, which take families away from home. The Sabbath was undoubtedly created for man and especially that he might rest and become renewed in spirit for his daily calling, but it was not for physical re-creation only but for spiritual renewal that it was ordained, and primarily for man's worship of God his Maker.

The Sabbath does not appear to have been kept in just the same strict way in the Early Church as it was in the Old Testament times. But the spirit of the Sabbath was kept, as shown by the disciples who came together to worship, for "the breaking of bread", and for fellowship in prayer. There seems to have come a new kind of liberty and joyfulness as the Sabbath became "the Lord's Day", a Day when Christians especially celebrated the Resurrection of Jesus, the seal of their salvation and redemption. As the Cross was ever to be remembered as the place of atoning sacrifice, where through His Blood Christ purchased for us entry into the Father's House, so the Lord's Day, the Day of our Lord's triumphant Resurrection from death and the grave, became the symbol of that Great Day of final emancipation when Christ will come again. How could the early Christians do other than hold that in constant memory out of sheer gratitude for what the Saviour had accomplished on behalf of mankind? This was an emancipation that had already begun to take place during the ministry of Jesus - as we see how Jesus, the Lord of the Sabbath, could walk through the cornfields with His disciples on the Sabbath Day, thus bringing down on Him the rebuke of the Pharisees who rejected Him. We read how on one occasion the disciples plucked the ears of corn and ate it to satisfy their hunger on the Sabbath, and Christ frequently healed the sick on the Sabbath. But on the Sabbath He also entered into the Synagogue to expound the Law and proclaim the Gospel. St Paul also, as we read, always made a point during his travels of entering into the local Synagogue on the Sabbath, and looked out for the place where prayer was wont to be made. Clearly the Sabbath Day was meant to be different from all the other days, the day when we take time to ponder how great is the salvation God has wrought for us, the day in which we can take time to feed upon the Bread of Life and tarry by living waters. It should be a day when we store up strength and courage for the warfare we wage during the week, and when faith becomes more certain through hearing the preaching of God's Word. It is surely obvious that this is a special day for the well-being of our children, that they may be built up in the knowledge and love of God, and be fortified with all possible spiritual equipment for life and the demands it will constantly be making on them. But parents must arrange for it, and do everything they can to make this possible. On no account must we distort the nature of the Sabbath or turn it into a Day of boredom! We may surely walk in the fields and by the sea shore. There are books that can be read, different from those of everyday, and games that can be played which are constructive and uplifting, or at least that do not run counter to the fact that the Lord's Day is different from the other days of the week.

It is a good thing to have special games, handiwork, as well as books that are kept for Sunday. If parents find a joy in going to Church, the children will doubtless find the same joy too. It is of course necessary for parents to set the example of attending Church. A thing that some of us have found helpful was to have discussions about the books of the Bible, Church History, the lives of the saints and missionaries, etc. To gather round the fireplace in winter or in the garden or in the park in summer brings the family together in a homely or home-like way, especially if the children are encouraged to take part and engage in the discussion themselves. A wise parent can decide how best to utilise this precious Day by infusing the right spirit into it, avoiding all "don'ts" as much as possible and yet finding an outlet for otherwise restrained energies. The main thing is to keep the spirit of the Day rather than make the letter of it repulsive.

"Honour thy father and thy mother." Few things are more distressing than to see people forsaking this commandment, and it now seems very common. One wonders how that ever came about. No doubt it is largely due to the wholesale departure from the Faith once committed to the saints. We call ourselves a

Christian nation, but, alas, these precepts that really make a Christian nation are brushed aside and forgotten. Children are quick to copy other children and when those children come from non-Christian homes the task of teaching the Christian way is much more difficult. We have seen how essential it is to teach obedience and respect to others and this has to be insisted on continually all through the school years. The slightest attitude of disrespect to either parent should always be dealt with at once and resisted by both parents. Respect toward others outside of the family should also be required, and this means that the parents must be careful not to criticise others before the child, or belittle them in any way. That the child should always honour his parents is an imperative from which there must be no deviation. To give way or ignore it will help the child to become defiant. Besides, it is one of those things of most importance in God's eyes, for if a child does not respect its parents whom it sees, how is it likely to respect God whom it does not see? Wrapped up in this respect for parents is reverence for God. The parent is the earthly representative of God and disrespect toward him or her is a grave fault.

If an ambassador to a country is snubbed or abused however slightly, it is gravely offensive to the country and the sovereign whom he represents. How much more, then, is it the case that when a child shows disrespect for the parents it is to be regarded as an offence against God? The parents' love for God, as for the child's eternal well-being, should be the prime reason why the parents should pay the utmost attention to this Commandment in respect of their own children. We are commanded throughout the Scriptures to have the rule over children in this matter. The earthly family is a reflection of the Heavenly Family and the laws are the same. It is my own belief that clear exposition of Biblical teaching in a winning and attractive way, as well as reasonable arguments for the kind of life to be lived toward God and man, will have their due effect and influence. Above all, the children will observe how far the parents themselves reverence the God whom they profess to serve, and how they show it in a practical way by being reverent in all their behaviour.

Closely attached to reverence toward God and to parents is a general reverence for others. Foolish jokes about biblical matters that even Christian people seem to indulge in at times, do much harm. Jokes about people, the crippled and the aged, the deformed and handicapped, bring down the judgment of God, for they are all forms of sinning against His Commandment. They violate the holiness and majesty of God as Lord and Creator of us all. His fiery judgment upon the disobedient, and irreverence in holy things, everywhere spoken of in the Scriptures was surely meant for our admonition and warning: God is always be the same, yesterday, today and for ever.

No children will ever be perfect and school children are not angels. All kinds of little quarrels, tiffs, unfairness, the misuse of each other's things, and misunderstandings, are bound to crop up in their little world. If a parent can turn all these things into the opportunity to apply the spirit of the Commandments and the Word of God, then a solid foundation will be laid which will stand the test out in the wider world in years to come. Much is said about getting on with one another among nations as among individuals, but much can be done in home and school to bring this about. It is easier to learn in the home and the school before people are caught up in the passions, greed, selfishness, and ambition pursued at others' expense that arise among the undisciplined and unbridled natures of people among whom they may have to live and work.

It is very sad that so many people do not value the Truth in the Holy Scriptures as they should, and do not take what the Bible says seriously enough. The written Word of God brings us the Truth for all time and can never be minimised. Even quite earnest Christians often do not take sufficient trouble to search out its treasure which is certainly not found on the surface. If it were, it would soon be abused, but it is there to be found by those who earnestly seek it - it is there for all who have eyes to see and ears to hear. For the Christian parent the Holy Scripture is a veritable mine of knowledge and wisdom, far outstripping every other source, for with its knowledge and wisdom comes power to bring to pass what it says. From the Word of God people can be given every kind of advice, and in it they will find the answer to many of their problems. This is of course a mystery to many, but it has been proved times without number. The Word of God works and works miraculously, which is proof of the divine inspiration of the Scriptures. The Word of God is the mightiest force in the world, the greatest blessing and the greatest comfort to those who believe it, but it can be a sledge hammer to those who reject it.

The living Voice of God that sounds through the Bible still speaks to God's people, and often in the most gentle tones of love to little children. I can recall a certain small school boy, who came to me more than once, saying, "I heard a little voice speaking to me. Do you think it was the voice of God?" I had no doubt it was, as subsequent experience proved. We adults are too materialistic and too preoccupied often with the daily business of living to hear that gentle Voice from the Heavenly Father to His children, or be moved by the soft zephyr breeze of the Spirit that "blows where it lists". How much we can miss that a little child receives! The radio transmits sounds and voices that encircle the earth, and to those whose ears are tuned in. Likewise there come to us from God messages that are, as it were, voiceless, and which, as St Paul once said, "It is not possible to utter". How much more, then, may the heart of a believing child tuned in to God the Father receive from Him through Jesus Christ, that Great Lover of little children!

The training of a child for God in the way that Christian parents would wish, means a life of faith for them too - faith in God and faith in a little child. "Without faith it is impossible to please God", and without it the Christian life is impossible. Apart from God we can do nothing, but with Him all things are possible. But we do our part and God does His. We pray daily for our children, but do we go away and forget what we have prayed for? Are our prayers mere words and form without action? We have to exercise our children in the daily walk of faith. God always honours a child's prayers, and sometimes encourages them "with signs following". It is always a joy and a privilege for a mother to pray with her child from its earliest years, but the child must be taught to pray on his own account. This helps much to take away the fear of God, and remove any sense of austerity that may lurk in his mind about God. It will bring a genuine awareness of God and enable him to become accustomed to depend on Him for all he needs. It is a good thing to teach a child to pray aloud and become accustomed to hearing his own voice in prayer. Sometimes adults have spoken to me about prayer, and on enquiry I have found out that they were actually afraid to pray, or that they did not know how to approach God and what words to use! This would never happen where a child has been taught to pray to God in much the same way as he asks his parents for the things he desires, and tells them everything that concerns him in a natural way. Prayer can be a comforting thing to a child, as many have experienced, and it will always remain in his inner consciousness throughout his life. A mother may feel too tired at night to be bothered, and it may need a special effort to pray with her child, but if she perseveres she will look back with gratitude to it in later years. A precious memory comes to my own mind of two small boys coming half way down the stairs and calling, "Mummy come up and pray with us". It is one of those precious moments that never fades. Children will naturally want to rely on their parent's prayers first, but gradually they will come to take their part along with their parents, and from there they will go on to pray on their own account. The example of our Lord in the matchless prayer of St John 17 teaches us how much prayer for us meant to Him. The disciples asked the Lord to teach them to pray, and shall we not teach our children to pray?

We have already spoken about reading the Bible, but this has also to be encouraged along with reading done in school. We teach a child to walk until it goes alone, and likewise we ought to teach our children to read and depend on God's Word until their use of it becomes quite natural. Some people think that the Bible is too hard and difficult for a child to read. Humanly speaking that may be so, but God means and asks that our children should be taught His Word, and He has His own way of interpreting it to them. God will scatter the crumbs they need and can assimilate, and the Holy Spirit will open their understanding little by little. Much could be said about this and demonstrated here, but that is not our intention now. We recall the story of Samuel, who must have been very young when God made Himself known to him, and we remember the account of our Lord at the age of twelve when he was found by His parents in the Temple "both hearing and asking questions and all who heard Him were astonished at His understanding". "Wist ye not that I must be about my Father's business?" He asked. We can safely leave a child in the hands of God the Holy Spirit to teach or to withhold all that a child is ready to know or not know. All Hebrew children were taught in their young years to memorise the Scriptures, although they did not understand them very well at the time. Chinese children used to memorise the classics of Confucius and other ancient writings at a very early age - no small task! Surely we as Christians should be as zealous as they! In the course of school days things won't always run smoothly. Progress at school may be slow and the teacher can be harassed and disappointed, while rebuke and discipline may have to be administered, and the child come home disconsolate. The parent may be tempted to judge the teacher harshly, but it is better to avoid doing so. It will not help at all if the child thinks his parent is against the teacher, and it may do harm. To make school a success the parent must as far as possible support the teacher, and refrain from criticism. The child may be at fault and if he thinks that his parent will champion him whether he is in the right or in the wrong which will have a warping effect on his mind. The better way is to help the child. School can be a miserable place if the child falls behind the other children in his lessons, but constant help can alter things very much. Some parents are loath to give the time, but when the happiness of the child is at stake the sacrifice ought to be made. With plenty of help and perseverance in explaining lessons the child will not only come to like school, but the bond between him and his parent will be deepened. Many children need personal help in the early years in addition to what they get at school, especially when they are slow to understand what is being taught to the whole class together, but when they once grasp the facts they will make quicker progress themselves. In this way problems can often be resolved away, rough places made plain and crooked places made straight - if the parents will only be concerned and take enough trouble.

Sooner or later children will learn other things at school than lessons. Little incidents will crop up which touch the sad and tragic side of life and perhaps the sordid as well. Children are apt to relate what happens in their own homes or things they have overheard in adult conversations. These may send a child anxiously to his parents for an explanation, and of course a satisfactory one should be given. The truth should never be avoided. But it is a good thing to steer a child away as far as possible from the things that are likely to depress and worry him. A bright side can generally be set against a darker one, and the mind kept from being burdened with such things unnecessarily before the time. It is good to encourage all children in sport and games at an early age. They will have to engage in all that at school of course and parents should do all they can to foster healthy open air activities of all kinds. It helps also to keep the mind healthy and occupied. School sports help to foster a team spirit which will stand a boy or girl in good stead throughout life. A child who merely stands on the touchline and does not take a full part with the others is likely to become sullen and difficult and perhaps introspective. Life will be hard and difficult for such a person when the time comes for him to mix in the everyday life of the working world. All children should be encouraged to take part in some school sport or some sort of team activity. The best men and women are generally those who have had a happy and carefree life in their early years. Plenty of activity keeps them healthy in every way, and as they grow in strength and knowledge they will be able to tackle the difficult problems of life all the better for having been free in their early days. School holidays offer a good opportunity for parents to share their life with their children. Walks in the country, or climbing mountains, picnics in the park or excursions to the seaside will keep children away from undesirable company and perhaps mischief, and the parents will reap much if they make themselves companionable to their children in the off school times.

As children continue at school and grow older it is important for the parents to "chum" them. More can be said about this in relation to the teenage years but it should be started at an earlier age if they want to influence their children and guide them into making right choices and drawing proper conclusions. Personally, it seems to me to be one of the clues to happy teenage years. As a child learns and increases in knowledge especially as he approaches the pre-teenage period he will continually want to communicate his knowledge, and it is a good opportunity for the parents to show a keen interest in all the child is reaching out after. In listening and sympathising and showing the spirit of comradeship rather than a spirit of superiority the parents will be able to steer the mind of their child unconsciously along the right track of healthy understanding. If a child feels he can come home and talk freely to his parents about things learned at school and can discuss matters with them in his own way, he will be relaxed and contented in his studies and be eager to unfold his ideas and discoveries, and the home will have an added attraction for him.

By being interested in the everyday things of school life the parents will be better able to encourage the spiritual progress of their children as well. Some people may be inclined to think that children do not have much inclination for spiritual things, but there is plenty of evidence for the opposite. They live no doubt in a kind of dream world which is quite natural before they come up against the realities of things. Through this dream world God often works in their minds laying foundations for realities. Little children often have incentives for good and perform little acts which demonstrate that God is working in their hearts. Memory brings back the picture of a little girl who on occasion would lay her hands across her mother's knees and say, "I want to be a good girl", apparently for no special reason. Children have a habit of comparing people with one another and on occasion a young girl asked if certain friends were really Christians. The mother was a little non-plussed and replied, "I think so". "Oh, I know", said the child, "their cup doesn't run over." Doubtless many people can recall such incidents that point to a child's thought of higher things. A child's mind seems always at work during the working hours and the parent can do much to contribute to its development in spiritual understanding. So many parents are not a little exercised over the young folk and one wonders if the earlier opportunities have been made as much of as they might have been.

The greatest thing in the world is love, taught St Paul. "Love suffers long and is kind; love envies not; love does not vaunt itself, is not puffed up, does not behave itself unseemly, seeks not its own, is not easily provoked, thinks no evil; rejoices not in iniquity, but rejoices in the truth; bears all things, believes all things, hopes all things, endures all things. Love never fails." Here, then, we have the perfect picture of what family life with our children should be. If our children can only absorb this kind of love, how much they will be saved from. The parents who seek to overcome and live this kind of love-life are those who will have the most influence over their children. As we ourselves practise the love of God in the home and demonstrate it in our family relations, so our children will understand God and be drawn to Him. We cannot hold them back for the time must come when they will be launched out into the world, but let us make sure as far as possible that we teach them, and make every possible use of the God-given opportunities for the training of our children, from the cradle on through the school years and perhaps even beyond.

7

The Teenage Years - Comrades

Little is said in the Holy Scriptures about "teenagers", but it has been a common-place expression in recent years. The teenage years are a period in a child's life when parents are anxious about them, especially in their later "teens". Some parents feel frustrated, perplexed, and disappointed. It arises no doubt from the age we live in. Things move fast, and the mind seems to be soon taken up with a vast number of things, for the world, as it were, puts its attractions in the front window. Ambitions arise from different motives than used to be the case, and the goals are different as well. Money is more to the foreground and the possibilities of a life of pleasure are within the grasp of many. Knowledge seems easier to acquire, and even if it is of a rather shallow sort it seems to serve the purpose of the day. The result is that the teenage years are apt to be a mixture of childhood and maturity, which has an unsettling effect and brings restlessness. Many of these young folk live in a world of fancy and hope about things which never come to pass. The impatience to be through with the plodding work of school life and then the realisation, sometimes too late, that without having all that the school offered they cannot succeed in their dreams. In some cases the short-cuts do appear to work for a year or two, and then after becoming disillusioned they begin to pick up the threads of study again and make good. Alas, many others lapse into an aimless state of mind. The desire to be out, earning money, and living a kind of life that seems to evade them, produce in many young people ambitions that are a real problem, not only to themselves, but to others, and particularly to their parents. Some people blame the radio and television for this; in so far as they hinder young people from using their brains and rob them of their power to concentrate on the individual pursuit of needful education, they certainly can be a hindrance. All this causes much anxiety to Christian parents, and much wisdom is needed which can be found in the Word of God.

Teenage troubles do not seem to appear in the Bible! At twelve or thirteen the Hebrew child was confirmed as a member of the covenant people of God. The redemption tax was to be paid from twenty years old and upward. At twenty young men could go forth to war; from twenty-five the Levites could take part in the Temple service, and at thirty priests could officiate in the Tabernacle or Temple. Our Lord returned to Nazareth from Jerusalem at the age of twelve and "was subject to his parents", but He did not begin His public ministry until He was thirty years of age. Although the Word of God does not change, yet the age does. There is the same God, the same Word and Saviour, but there is a new and a different world. The wonder of the Word is that it fits into every age. It is still needed in every age, and remains the one true source where all can find the true way of living and the life everlasting. "To whom shall we go?" asked Peter, "You have the words of eternal life."

When a child enters secondary school at the age of eleven or twelve, things begin to change. The demands made for study and application, the further fields of learning, and instruction in the history of the nations, politically and racially, all have a part in developing the child's mental capacity. Knowledge has advanced so rapidly and ever-increasing discoveries and empirical scientific developments keep the mind in a perpetual state of advance. There are other things too. The newspapers, periodicals, and educational programmes through radio and television crowd the life and thought with so much new knowledge to assimilate that one may well feel a lifetime has been lived in those years compared with what used to happen even fifty years ago! Naturally the impact of all this upon teenagers brings about a drastic change in their outlook on life, and must have a variable effect upon them. In the first two years this may not be so apparent.

Things change a little in the home as well, though not perceptibly during the first part. Here, then, is the challenge to parents. Hitherto they have been the guides, the planners. The reins of government have been undisputed in their hands, and home has been a happy place, undisturbed by what now looms ahead. By nature most of us are loath to have change, especially in the inner circle of the family. We want our children to grow up but we dislike them to grow away from the simplicity and trustfulness of childhood. As the boys grow into manhood, and the girls show signs of maturing into womanhood, mothers especially have their heart-pangs, and feel a little apprehensive. What then shall we do? The best and wisest thing is for us to accept it. If we continually view things with fears, forebodings and regrets, we shall entirely lose out. Those who are earnest Christians and desire above all else that their children shall be won for the Lord for all time, will keep the importance of persevering in a spiritual approach to all things, at all times, always to the fore. For the sake of our children, then, we too must change in certain directions.

It is very important to retain the confidence of our young folk. As we have hitherto taken the initiative in making decisions, so now we should begin to encourage the children to make their own decisions, and to help them as far as possible to take the right stand under their own convictions of what is best and noblest. As we have tried to emphasise, much now depends on what has gone before, and how wisely we have used every opportunity in the formative years. In any case, we must change our own attitude with our fast-growing children. Some parents, partly out of fear no doubt, take up a restrictive outlook about various things, and even try to force through their own ideas. To do that is likely to provoke opposition, which, even if it be in a mild form at first, may increase and cause much unhappiness. Decisions have to be made all through life; and guidance and understanding at this time will make a great difference later on. We need to foster a feeling of oneness with our children, so that they will feel free to discuss the various problems that come up from day to day. We have to aim at comradeship with our young folk, although in such a way that this does not appear forced. It reminds me of a remark made by a person in Shanghai to a young English woman who had married a Scotsman. "The way to get on", she said, "is to let the husband think he is getting his own way, even though it may not in fact be the case!"

As parents we shall doubtless have to sacrifice some of our former notions, although not our principles. We shall have to be interested in things that do not really appeal to us, and we shall have to give of our time to them, which may make the greatest demands on us. So many parents become rather alienated from their children as they advance in their teens, and have little in common with them. It is not that they wished it to be so or had consciously caused it, and they can hardly tell how it has come about. Most of these difficulties are the outcome of a wrong start. Experience teaches that where parents have been comrades and friends with their children, things have gone better. If we have already trained them along the right way of good living from the earliest days the likelihood is that they will make right decisions and take right attitudes toward things now of their own accord. This may sound rather subtle, but actually it is the way God works with us. For instance, God gives us His commands in His Word, the "thou shalt" and "shalt not", etc. He teaches us what He expects from us. His Word and precepts provide the criteria for our daily walk. As someone has put it, "He uses many methods by which to gain our confidence and love". We are also given in the Epistles of the New Testament very full accounts of how we should live and act all our days. Yet God does not drive, force or coerce us. He leaves us to decide, to follow Him and abide in Him. Is it not like that between us and our children? We must do all we can through prayer, by teaching the Word, and by setting an example in our own lives. It is by following His pattern closely, and keeping to the way He teaches and in which He leads us, that we may expect Him to do for us and our children what we cannot do for ourselves or apart from Him. Like God, as we do our part continually in practical as in spiritual matters, we must be careful, as it were, to keep ourselves out of sight.

There are many opportunities in which we can resort to the "many methods" to bring about success. We must adopt a "give and take" approach. For instance, we can consult our children and ask their advice about real problems, as well as about simple ordinary matters about the house, dress, etc, and in this way prevent barriers and conflicts arising, for it is in these small things that the seeds of difference can germinate. It is a good thing for a mother to take up the attitude of an elder sister at times. Our Lord often asked His disciples what they thought, and drew from them their ideas in such a way that He could use them unobtrusively to indicate a better way. We can disarm children's anxieties when in various ways they may feel awkward and out of place, as when we have adult friends visiting us, or when we visit others or attend various gatherings. It is this atmosphere of "chumminess" that will set the family at ease, and make them relaxed and natural. If done in the right spirit and way it will bring much joy to the parents as well as new interests.

It is unfortunate that some parents persist so long in not recognising that their children are ceasing to be just children, and that they are emerging into adulthood. This intermediate stage is not only difficult for the parent, but it is a strain on the young folk as well. Some children mature more quickly than others, girls sooner than boys as a rule. Circumstances should be allowed to guide a wise parent. One of the things that makes fellowship pleasant among friends is the fact that they respect each other, with their different views, outlooks, tastes, etc. That is also needful in a family. Parents ought to cultivate this feeling of mutual respect as far as possible. Our young folk will say and discuss things that may seem rather stupid at times to us who know so much. But here we need patience and to remember that though they are moving away from childhood, they may be childish for quite a long time in certain directions. A parent must be careful not to slip into the temptation to make fun of a child, or to expose his ignorance, or for the parent to appear superior. Every boy or girl has to feel his or her way gradually into adult life. This growing up is a progressive thing, and takes time, and often much has to be learned through bungling and stumbling, and sometimes things have to be unlearned or re-learned as time goes on. It is, however, in this way that we all learn, and sympathetic understanding is needed, when sometimes silence is best, and when advice or guidance may be given in a way that does not cause embarrassment to the less well informed. In all this we need much wisdom, and to remember the Word that says, "If any of you lack wisdom, let him ask of God, who gives to all liberally, and upbraids not, and it shall be given him." It is interesting to notice that God does not upbraid us for our stupidity and ignorance. To be true ambassadors for Him we must not do so either.

Our chief business is to make home all that it should be during these important years. Our teenager will naturally form new friendships at school. Few can choose the type of school and school environment they wish these days. Children will want to bring their friends home and in this matter we can help, and perhaps, guide as well. We all know that friendships formed in these early years have influence for good or otherwise, sometimes lasting a lifetime. Much tact will be needed to influence our children in the right direction. We must make them feel that they have the freedom of the home in this way, so that they will enjoy bringing back their friends. The parents can then find out if a friendship is helpful or not and patiently steer them in the best direction. We must be careful, of course, not to betray our unfavourable impressions in a dominating way, as that might mean that undesirable friendships will be pursued outside the home and without the parents' knowledge. Given time an undesirable friendship may fade away of its own accord. Some children, as one writer has expressed it, "possess the secret of spiritual growth", and if we have persevered in teaching them the Word of God, we can have faith that this will work out in our children as the need arises. But it is our duty to try to arrange that the right kind of children and friends frequent our homes and mingle with our family. Where there is a family of boys and girls this is generally easier. For one thing they have each other to discuss with and entertain, and often they keep each other in order! But it is good for parents to suggest that their children should invite other Christian children to the home and in that way foster a circle of friends.

One is very often weary of the emphasis put on so-called teenagers. They are referred to as something apart from the ordinary run of human beings, and are often held in awe! To take up this attitude would foster the thought that it is expected, or at least that it is anticipated, that they should constitute a group separate from others. It is painful to see how in many cases these young folk go off with their special friends, even to Church, as well as to their recreative pursuits. The parents feel they are not wanted or show marked indifference to this kind of thing. It may have rather harmful results in some respects. For one thing it produces a very selfish attitude toward those to whom they owe most. It tends to foster a spirit of separation which impoverishes life in every way, and in the end brings much unhappiness. There are times, of course, when it is right for the young folk to go off on their own, but when separation goes too far it destroys family fellowship and wounds the love there. It breeds conceit and betrays a mistaken view of youth as being a kind of climax instead of an interim period in life. One of its miserable evils is that it makes too marked a division between the young and the old, through which they both suffer. Both have much to contribute to each other, and in that way character is formed. The world outside the home is also like a family, and it needs all ages to make a happy and harmonious one. The old can certainly gain much from the young who are stepping out into the fast-changing world of today, and the old can pass on rich experience which can no doubt be of great help to the younger people. Unhealthy division has entered into so much private and public life of late, generating all kinds of bitterness and resentment. We hear on many sides how the young throw off all responsibility toward the old and aged even in material respects. Add to this a lack of understanding, love, helpfulness and solicitude toward the frail members of the family and it sours not only the family itself but the world in which we live day by day. Family age distinctions of this sort are not found in the Holy Scriptures. The family is the home. Israel, the Chosen people, were regularly spoken of as a unit. The Christian Church is the same; it is made up of old and young, weak and strong, female and male, and little children. The Church is one and should be, and so must the true family be. Serious departures have been made from the Scriptures to the deterioration of modern society everywhere. A College lecturer recently remarked, "We need to talk ourselves into the Bible"; and we also need to talk the Bible back into ourselves and into our homes.

The aim of the Christian parent should be to maintain this unitary conception of the family. It makes for real joy and surely it can be done by the parents themselves growing up, again, as it were, along with their children. The father can help a lot at this stage. Boys need their father's understanding as girls need their mother's. Sometimes fathers seem to stand aloof from their boys in such a way that no confidence develops between them during these most important years. The boy seems to fear and stand in awe of the father and the father appears to mistrust his son, so that they grow apart, the father becoming cynical and the son coming to regard his father with contempt or just to disregard him. Boys need their father's companionship. He should be an elder brother joining in all their pursuits as much as possible or at least showing a keen interest in all they do. A family whom I know very well, comes to my mind, where the father is actually a real companion to his sons in many ways. During holidays and at other times he is their chief companion. They play football, golf, and cricket and enjoy sailing and swimming together, to the great pleasure of all. The boys love to have their father with them and many times when he would rest or sleep, it is "come on, father, do come", and he goes. The boys love it as they do him. Indoors they

The Teenage—Comrades

sometimes play chess and other games and each and all take a keen interest in all adventures and scientific discoveries and so on. Their father is a beloved chum and of course, along with the mother, takes a deep interest in their daily school home-work. They are all true believers in God's Word, and show the fruit of it in their lives. Surely there could be many more such happy families, but it needs both parents to be of one heart and mind, and not least the presence and impetus of the Holy Spirit. Another incident shows much the same conception in the mind of a young girl who some years ago, then in her teens, went to visit an aunt who had just come to live in the same town. The aunt asked the young girl if she had something she would like to confide in her that she could not confide in her mother, as that had frequently happened in her own family. "Oh", said the girl, "I always tell my mother everything; there is nothing that I would not tell my mother." The mother, on hearing about this conversation from the aunt herself, surely felt intensely happy at her daughter's trust in her. Should we not all work to that end with our boys and girls? Parents may feel they have not the time to go all out in maintaining confidential relations with their offspring; it certainly does take time, but when we consider how much is at stake and how soon the opportunity may be gone, would it not be better to forgo spending time on other things less important in the long run? It is not enough to cater for food, dress, and physical health and comfort, and pay little attention to the lasting things of life, the spiritual welfare of our children. It is only too possible that they may run to seed if we neglect them.

We will wake up to find that our children, while they bear considerable likeness to us in many ways, beside physical features, are nevertheless quite different. They have different characteristics, tastes, and ideas. They like things that don't appeal to us to any extent. Some are more thoughtful and meditative, while others are more constantly on the move. As they grow these contrasts become more evident. We cannot expect our children to be identical with ourselves. Again and again they will make quite different choices from what we would have done, especially as they become older. It will help us if we remember that each one of our children is an individual personality, with responsibilities entirely his or her own. In God's sight they are all individual souls who have to be saved individually for Him. They are fitted for their place in the world with capacities given to them by God, and to Him they will have to give an account of how they have used them. They have not only to go out into the world in due time to work and to establish their own homes, but they are spiritually answerable to God over accepting His provision for their salvation, or in rejecting it. As parents we have to consider this thoroughly and allow them to live up to the light and understanding they have and not to count on their parents' profession of faith as their own, nor feel forced to adopt the same approach in everything, especially in non-essential matters. Their character has to be developed and strengthened so that they can stand alone, as they will certainly have to do in due course. But in all this we can seek to help without usurping what is their own. It is of course by trying out things, testing, meeting temptations and resisting them, that their life is made what it really is.

In choosing a career or in preparing for one a young person must be allowed to follow his or her own bent. It has been shown many times how unwise it is for a parent to bring pressure to bear on young folk in this regard. The children of missionaries sometimes grow up with the idea that it is expected of them that they too should be missionaries. Cases of this kind have been known to me and in some instances it has not worked out well at all. Young men have gone into the ministry because their parents wished them to do so, and it has turned out a failure. Girls have been pushed into nursing or teaching and boys have been expected to carry on the business of their father to which they have an aversion, and the lives of these young people have not turned out to be as happy as they might have been. The main thing for the parents to do is to point out that the wisest course at the end of the day is for young people to do what they feel is meant for them, in accordance with God's judgment for them. We cannot as Christians force our children into Christ's work but it is our duty to do all we can to help them take up work that will be honouring God and not lead them into the company of those who are godless. Many young people have decided ideas of their own at an early age about what they intend to do, while others are longer in making a decision and continue to be undecided too long to fit themselves for anything definite - in such a case it may well be helpful for the parents to offer them some advice. I well remember speaking to one of my own boys in his early teens about his career. Along with others he had been asked by his master what he was thinking of preparing for. I ventured a suggestion, but was promptly answered, "But my mind was made up long ago", and he set out to do what he had in mind, which is no doubt what he was fitted for.

There is a danger in some homes for the children to be too sheltered from the hard spots of life. This may be desirable in the early years, but as they advance into their teens it is necessary for them to be prepared for the eventualities that overtake us all at times, and to breed that sympathetic spirit for others that is always so important. Years ago I recall reading in the Life of Catherine Booth, whose home was then in London, how she decided that her children should know something of the conditions in which many people had to live. She arranged for her children to visit some of the slums of the city and show sympathy by distributing packets of tea and useful things to the needy folk who lived in so much squalor. None of us should ever hide ourselves from the needs of others and what we owe to our fellow human beings. Another true story comes to my mind of a small boy who saw a man dead drunk lying on the pavement. It was a shock to the child, and it had to be explained to him that the poor man had fallen into the temptation of taking too much strong drink. The boy was greatly impressed for some time, and then announced to his family that when he became a man he was going to be a preacher to save the "drunk man". Actually that boy is now a preacher and seeks to minister the Gospel of salvation from sin. Today young people learn the same things in other ways, for life now seems more public with the information broadcast through radio and television, and parents themselves are rather different in their outlook. Christian parents will naturally want to guide their children in these matters. No one thinks of putting a boat out to sea before it is fitted to withstand the storms and made shock-proof against the battering of the waves. We cannot expect our young folk to weather the storms of life without adequate preparation and equipment.

    A minister recently remarked that "the hardest challenge to youth today is met when they leave school, and sometimes their homes as well, and go out into the world to earn their way in office, shop or factory, and sometimes find there a morally putrid atmosphere." Some succumb immediately, but some struggle through and stand upright. The same can be said of many of our young folk who have to serve in the forces whether in times of war or peace. Many young men who had intended entering the ministry of the Church or some other profession returned home entirely changed in outlook and intention. This is one of the many problems that face parents today and drives them to prayer. Yet we cannot forget how God does His work for those who completely put their trust in Him. Many parents can witness to the wonderful way in which God's skilful hands have guided the youth committed to Him in faithful and continual prayer. He can and does devise means for His loved ones. At the same time we must try to do all we can in directing the course of our young folk, maybe indirectly, to the kind of work, office, workshop or whatever, where we know there are the Lord's people working and whose influence will be helpful. It needs both father and mother to tackle this responsibility of preparing our children so that they may not leave us to go forth into the world blind and ignorant. Some parents trust that their children will find their way alright without any special help. Others are reticent and excuse themselves from such responsibilities. But if the future of our sons and daughters is bound up in our love, we must surely do our utmost, whether by listening to them, by informing, warning or advising them. We have to try every way in which to help them, apart from exerting force upon them. The knowledge of a happy home in the background can do so much. The cords that bind there will bear the strain of many a pull, and sustain many a baffled spirit. During the last war a young Christian man was conscripted into the army and sent to India. The atmosphere on the troop ship was a shock and made him sick at heart. He wrote home saying that one night he felt greatly cast down and went up on deck to be alone and while leaning over the rails and looking into the darkness he felt utterly miserable, until his thoughts turned back to his home. As he thought of his loved ones there he suddenly felt fresh strength and courage and a deep sense stole over him that they were praying for him. A closer atmosphere was around him than the one he had loathed, and the next day he discovered there were other young men like himself with whom he was able to have Christian fellowship to the end of the voyage. Great weapons of spiritual power are in the hands of Christian parents - why should they remain dormant?

A good deal of harm may be done to our teenager, more than we realise, through criticism in the home and among members of the family. This has already come before us, but it is something that grows in importance as the children get older. Few things can have a more deadly and poisoning effect on the mind. It is a common fault among us and we are all guilty of it at one time or another. To discuss our friends in a critical or judgmental way, the minister, the teacher or anyone else, is not only damaging to them but to ourselves also. From God's point of view, it is sin. We have no right to judge others in this way and especially those who profess to belong to the family of our Lord. How often when we have had hard critical thoughts about a certain person we have found out that very person had a hidden sorrow, a serious handicap in life or a difficult situation in which to live. We cannot read another's thoughts and know their fears and struggles, and we can know nothing of their temptations. Society can be very cruel, even Christians. Often people who have hardships and difficulties try to hide them from others by doing things they are not meant to do or saying things they had no thought of saying; and in attempts to camouflage their problems they unintentionally lay themselves open to condemnation by being critical of others when they do not deserve it. "Love thinks no evil", neither should we. "Love covers a multitude of sins", and faults, many of which we ourselves are guilty as we know well in our own hearts. How healing can be the Pauline words, "Who is he who condemns? It is Christ who died?" All flippant jokes and criticisms or smart remarks about others are harmful to our young folk. They cannot assess a situation and it draws their attention to many things that may never have entered their minds, and induces them to exercise their imaginations in unprofitable ways. Many a school teacher has had her life made miserable by criticism at school and in the home. To be honest we must admit that criticism is seldom truthful, and it increases in untruthfulness as it spreads. The same can be said of what goes on in the office or workshop. Some years ago I knew of a schoolboy who was sent to a boarding school, and whose mother was a friend of mine. He was an only child and may have appeared spoilt because he had not roughed it. In time his life was made so miserable by the other children that it told on his health for years, as a result of which he developed a complex which made it difficult for him to mix with others. It was sad and need never have happened. Criticism in the home can cause that kind of thing. Young children and young folk can be very cruel to one another and make life intolerable unless they are taught in the home the horribleness of it and they learn from the Word of God to love their neighbours as themselves. There is a constructive criticism which can be helpful and building. But otherwise we should regard criticism of the censorious sort as rank poison in the home where it so easily occurs and grows up often without our being aware that we are being critical.

Some parents have found it necessary to accustom themselves to become good listeners! Our young folks often go over and over things and demonstrate to us much that we know ourselves but which they take for granted that we do not know. To listen and show interest, as if it were new to us begets that coveted thing, sympathy and understanding, in which we also show our appreciation of others. Everything new to them will naturally, they think, be new to everyone else. It is always fatal to insert our knowledge of it in a way that will rob them of their own discovery. We can make our own contributions, of course, but we must let them take the initiative. They are feeling their way into new knowledge and nothing helps them so much as being able to express themselves in their own way. The Apostle James once wrote, "Let every man be swift to hear and slow to speak." It is a good maxim to adopt sometimes, so that the young folk can say all they wish to say. Sometimes when the parents have proved themselves trustworthy, they become a kind of repository, by being trusted with secret thoughts and plans. It brings great rewards which extend into the future. The thing that is often greatly in demand is "a heart at leisure from itself", whether to soothe and sympathise, or to be open to receive confidences and ideas which others wish to work out. The world would be a sweeter place, and the home more heavenly, if we all had time, and made time, to hear and enter into the difficulties and problems that baffle so many others, even though it is only by listening and silent assent. If we are wise we shall never project our own superior knowledge (as we imagine it to be) upon our children or the friends they bring around us, for it will act like a blight on the opening flowers of youth and stultify growth. The young folk of today have to learn and meet much that was not deemed necessary when we were young. Modern education will keep them abreast of the times. The parents who are alive to situations will feel that they too have to learn and will enjoy learning things over again as well as quite new things in order to keep pace with the development of their children. There has always been something new and life has always seemed to have plenty of thrills in which the comradeship of one's children is the spice of life.

We cannot but continue to reiterate the prime need constantly to allow the Word of God to guide and lead us in the Christian life. It is the source of all we need. Without it we cannot have faith. For as one writer said, "faith takes holds of the Word of God and faith brings hope", and again "faith takes hold of the Word of God and rests upon it". While our children are still with us and as yet in their teens, we have great opportunities for fellowship with them in the life of faith. We can have round table talks in which they take part in discussion with the whole family. The facts of life are beginning to loom up and fresh insights into the application of the Word of God are needed. If the child has been well acquainted with the Scriptures from his earliest days the Word of God is more likely to become flesh and blood and to take on a new vitality for him, speaking to him in a form that finds its way with conviction into the heart. Children who have thus been taught will likely turn to this Word of God when faced with challenges from the outside. The case of a young boy who had not been very long in high school comes to mind. He came home one day rather perturbed in mind. Things had been taught at school by one of the masters which ran counter to faith, and the boy's belief in the Word of God had to withstand the attack. Happily he was led to a certain passage of Scripture which completely satisfied him and which met the precise case so clearly that he was convinced and remained so. Without doubt the Holy Spirit came to his aid and gave the necessary understanding and illumination in answer to his own believing heart, but his familiar knowledge of the Scripture made that the more possible and likely. A few years later a younger brother of his returned from school with a similar challenge. It was very disturbing, but again the knowledge of God and His Word came to the rescue and won out effectively. One wonders what happens to those boys who have no knowledge of the Word, and know very little of God. Are they swept away from faith to rest on some changing hypothesis and finally lapse into unbelief? It is not enough for parents to rely on Sunday School, Bible class or even the minister. Nothing can quite take the place of the home in which the Word of God is honoured, believed, and loved.

Some people argue that the Word of God as we have it in the Bible is uninviting and uninteresting to young folk. Outwardly it may appear so to some, and often also to older folk. The truth is that they have never got inside the Word. The Bible is rather like the picture we are given of the ancient Tabernacle, or the Tent of meeting with God, which was erected in the wilderness march of Israel to the promised land. The outer covering was black and unattractive, made of goats' hair. But the inside was rather different. There was a covering of gold, and the atmosphere within was that of fragrant incense and rare perfume made from special kinds of spice prepared by the apothecary and not allowed to be imitated. That is a picture of the Bible to those who have managed to get inside it. The Pearl of great price is to be found there. Nowhere else can the forgiveness of sins be found, and nowhere else is the Cross understood and manifested. Through the veil we see the Great City and the gates that are never shut to those who earnestly seek to enter. Where else can such comfort be found, and such hope be inspired and faith become so real?

There are many problems facing Christian parents which are difficult to solve apart from the miracle of the Word of God. All are not cast in the same mould and the aptitude for spiritual receptiveness varies. Parents may worry because their young folk take up different attitudes to what they have done. This becomes very real in some families as the young folk near the end of their teens. They may be quite earnest in their Christian profession, take part in Church activities, teach in Sunday School and so on, but their everyday life is difficult. It is hard for them to escape doing things that vex the feelings of their parents, and quite unwittingly friction may arise. How, they may ask, are they to cope with these things? It is in fact a common question which regularly turns up in Christian discussions. Quite clearly these young people have to live and work in a different world from that which their parents lived in, and some consideration must be given to that fact. Young folk do not like to be thought different or peculiar. Some may feel that it lets their Christian witness down to be different and they do not want to be treated adversely by those who employ them. Life may be drab and monotonous and they react to other things that stimulate and engage their active natures. We cannot escape realising that life for these young folk has entirely changed from what it was, and we have to take much for granted that makes us feel anxious. It is no use criticising or nagging, which parents in their panic are tempted to do. It is best to ignore our immediate reactions as much as possible and try to look at things from their angle. Nor is it any use looking miserable and unhappy about things, as this will only make for barriers between parents and their young people. When properly thought out things may not seem so bad as we may be tempted to think. How far do these things really matter? Do any of them really hinder the spiritual life, or are our reactions not being governed by man-made tradition? It is important that we do not fall into the error of the Pharisees, who were continually accusing the Lord of the way He and His disciples behaved, in breaking the Sabbath Day, eating with sinners and tax-gatherers, having meals without washing hands, cups and other utensils. They fussed over petty things and the Lord answered them by pointing out how they substituted the tradition of the Elders for the Word of God. Many of them may have been as earnest about keeping the legal requirements as St. Paul was before his conversion, but they were mistaken in their zeal. Christ taught that faith in Him as the Son of God and the Saviour of mankind made people free. We remember how the Apostles made decrees that freed the Gentile believers from the burdens of the Old Jewish laws. May it not be possible for older Christians to put a yoke on the necks of the younger ones? As parents we may have to adapt ourselves to new conditions.

As we look back over the years we cannot but realise how things have changed and how things that used to shock in the past are now taken for granted, and now few people think anything about them, such as changes in dress and hair-styles! These are not matters that Christians should really be troubled about. Certainly we must not let changes in customs of that kind come between us and our children. What matters is the heart. They have lived in the midst of change and they naturally see things somewhat differently. We must rather follow the rule, "In all things essential, unity, in things not essential, liberty." Let us, then, be liberal in thought toward our young folk in all unessential matters. If it costs us to part with prejudices, is it not worthwhile if we gain the salvation of our children? All generations pass through different phases, many of which fade away as the more solid things are attained. We can always afford to wait for the turning of the tide! The really important thing is to let love have its preeminence over everything we think and do. The Apostle John wrote to little children, parents and young people alike: "Love not the world, neither the things that are in the world; if any man love the world, the love of the Father is not in him. Beloved let us love one another. God is love."

8

The Straying Sheep - Faith Undaunted

In his Epistle to the Romans St Paul gives us an immortal picture of Abraham, "Who against hope believed in hope...He staggered not at the promise of God through unbelief." It is helpful for us often to recall the marvellous faith of these early "fathers of the Faith".

God made great promises to Abraham, although throughout his life he saw hardly a vestige of the likelihood of their ever being fulfilled. God seemed to demand much from him in every way, and we are told that Abraham believed God's Word and went on in faith, with no substance as it were on which to rest his faith. Numbers of years evidently elapsed even between the times that God spoke to him so that it might have been thought that God had forgotten him, and left him to wander in a strange land alone. Nevertheless, Abraham held on tenaciously, without faltering or even staggering. God had said, "Walk before me and be thou perfect", and Abraham obeyed and walked before the Lord. He was not discouraged because of hope deferred, never calculating, not counting the cost, not murmuring, nor for one moment entertaining the thought that God would fail to do what he had promised. So, although God had promised that his seed would be as the sand on the seashore and the stars for their multitude, and that they would inherit the land in which Abraham spent his days, yet he never owned a piece of ground except the cave of Machpelah in which Abraham was laid to rest beside Sarah his wife. In the New Testament our Lord confirmed the faith of Abraham when He said "Abraham saw my day and rejoiced". The faith of Abraham pierced, as it were, the very heavens and he saw God's secret that He would one day come to this earth in the manhood of Christ who would be born of the seed of Abraham. He did not let temporal promises and blessings obscure the greater blessing of the everlasting Kingdom and the supreme victory of Christ over all nations and peoples. Truly Abraham was of those "who looked for a city which has foundations, whose builder and maker is God". "He endured as seeing him who is invisible", and God made him the father of the Faith, the father of all who believe in Jesus Christ as their Saviour. What an example we have before us! How does our puny faith measure up to that of Abraham? Let us take time to dwell on it whenever we feel overcharged and overcast.

Let us take a glimpse of Isaac and Jacob also. Isaac followed in the footsteps of his father. Even though God appeared to him in a lesser way, nevertheless Isaac steadfastly clung to the promises of God made to Abraham and wandered about hardly finding a resting place for his family and cattle, yet never complaining but always accepting what God gave him or what God denied him or withheld from him. He lived a surrendered life, firmly holding to the promise that one day would be fulfilled, although not in his own lifetime. In Jacob we have a different character, one often overwhelmed with trouble and borne down with fear, although sometimes it was brought on by his own shortcomings. We can see many likenesses in him to ourselves - so often bargaining with God, suspicious of his children who were not faithful, careful for his living and his substance. Often he seemed to plan his own life and forget God, until God called him to a halt with some catastrophe which drove him back to Him. How human he was! One of the most comforting verses is to be found in Isaiah where God, says, "Fear not thou worm Jacob"! Does God take care of worms of the dust such as we are? Yes indeed, for He said at the same time, "Fear not, I will help you

The Straying Sheep—Faith Undaunted

saith the Lord and thy Redeemer, the Holy One of Israel". This same Jacob also held on, in spite of everything that would overwhelm him in the world, to the faith and promises given to faithful Abraham. He rose to great heights before God and God also loved him and made him a prince in Israel for ever, and gave him special revelations as we find when in his old age on his deathbed he prophesied that the Lawgiver and the Sceptre would not depart from the tribe of Judah until the Messiah should come, unto whom would be the gathering of the people.

This is the kind of faith we are called on to emulate in our own pilgrimage. It is the faith that St Paul and St Peter and the other Apostles set before them as their example. They trod the same pathway, they suffered, were persecuted and hounded from place to place and had no secure place in which to live. They were often in prison and in banishment; they suffered death and endured as seeing Him their Saviour and Lord who had said unto them, "You are my friends if you do whatsoever I command you", and who when He set His face steadfastly toward the Cross, said, "Follow me." The Early Church was born in the hot fires of persecution. In reading the accounts of those days one marvels that any Church should be born and stand and withstand in the face of all that came upon it. Those early Christians also went on in faith, feeding on the Word of God, and believing all things, hoping in the fulfilment of all things that the Lord had said, yet seeing only suffering, death and worse, of whom the world is not worthy.

In meditating upon all this we come to think of the children over whom so many parents are broken in heart. Things have not turned out as they had prayed and hoped for, and they are overwhelmed, amazed and perplexed. Faith is being sorely tried when it is a case of having to follow blindly, scarcely knowing where they are going each step of the way. Most of us doubtless have known some of the great saints who followed the Lord and yet whose cup became bitter because of one of their own children who had gone into the far country. Some of these saints have indeed been called to drink that cup to the very dregs. Others have had children born to them who are deformed in some way or other and the care of them has become a very heavy burden coupled with fear about what is to happen and who is going to care for them after they themselves have passed on. These are but a few of the afflictions that may come on believing parents.

One has heard it said, "Why did God allow this?" "I cannot understand." The heart is numbed with a pain that cannot find relief anywhere, a burden that cannot be laid down, perhaps until death. Many are perplexed and wonder how these things can be. To the Christian the problem is greatest for the fear nags at the heart that somehow something has not been right between themselves and their Lord. They may have left something undone that they ought to have done, or they may have done something that they ought not to have done. Thus temptation assails them from one quarter after another. Of course there may in some cases be a realisation that things might have been done differently. This may be the case with some children who have been left in the home country when their parents were abroad, and who in the course of the years have gone far from any Christian profession. On the other hand, some children left at home have followed in the footsteps of their parents in the walk of faith and have been a joy to the heart of their parents. We have for the most part to look elsewhere for the reason why God has permitted such a great trial to come to certain saints.

Grace is not inherited. We can see that from many instances recorded in the Holy Scriptures. Our children are individual persons and responsible characters and stand in relation to God as those who must themselves accept Him as Lord and Saviour or do otherwise. We cannot think of them as in any way favourites with God. None of us may expect any special privilege because we have believed and sought to follow the Lord all our life. We may sometimes get into a state of mind in which we are apt to count too quickly and too lightly on God's doing everything for us that we desire, whether we ask Him or not. We are all rather likely unconsciously to adopt such an attitude. God permits many things to happen to us apart altogether from the care of our children: deep sorrow, unutterable and baffling trials that weigh us down well nigh to the grave. God chastens every believer and none escapes. We cannot choose the form which our chastisement will take. He who is all wise and who knows our hearts and lives better than ourselves will choose that for us. We would fain escape all sore experiences, especially the chastisement which makes us suffer hard and long. We find it difficult to accept it from Him who loves us. Yet it is part of our life's discipline if we are to be chiselled, moulded and shaped to adorn the heavenly Temple which is lightened by the Lamb of God. We are to be prepared for life with Him and it is essentially by way of the Cross, that we may not be condemned with the world but be made ready for that which "eye has not seen nor ear heard, neither has entered into the heart of man, the things which God has prepared for them who love Him".

Affliction is part of God's plan for His redeemed and is a sign that we are His and that He is working out His own pattern in our lives and hearts. He sees the end from the beginning. He sees the complete pattern and knows the service it is meant to render. We look at the mass of the tangled threads in the tapestry of our lives and feel confused and hopeless, and are baffled at the apparent lack of any necessity for it. It leads nowhere, we think, but God, blessed be His name, thinks otherwise. To have a right outlook upon things is essential in the Christian way of life. For the Christian nothing is aimless, nothing without meaning and significance in God's eyes. That is the comforting thought. One of old said, "Thou knowest the way I take and when I am tried, I shall come forth as gold". Dare we believe that God knows and has a reason for everything in your life and mine? He promises that He will keep us as the apple of His eye. Can the slightest affliction that overtakes us fail to touch Him? Rather does He know beforehand and waits to see how our faith reacts to Him. He who cares for the fall of one sparrow, who counts the hairs of the head, He who was so careful that the fragments of bread should be picked up that nothing may be lost, will He permit anything to touch His beloved trusting child without it being in some mysterious way His permission for us?

The secret of peace in all such afflictions is to accept it from Him. To doubt or rebel, or find another reason for them is to add to our suffering. If we are truly His, then everything that touches us touches Him. "Take my yoke upon you and learn of me, and you shall find rest to your souls." To accept, to bow meekly and take it from the Lord and then to look up and cast all our burdens on Him is really what He expects and waits for. The Lord will not put upon us any more than we are able to bear even though the load may seem intolerable at times, for if we accept what comes as His yoke then somehow in His own way He will make it light enough for us to carry. In the midst of it all we shall have the unclouded consciousness of nothing between Him and ourselves. Otherwise if we refuse to take it in this way we shall be continually chastening our own spirits and tormenting ourselves until we sink down into a state of hopelessness. "Beloved, think it not strange concerning the fiery trial which is to try you as though some strange thing happened to you, but rejoice inasmuch as you are partakers of Christ's sufferings, that when his glory will be revealed, you may be glad also with exceeding joy." St Peter wrote these words not long before he was himself to suffer the death, if tradition is correct, on a cross in his old age.

To resist God brings endless pain and misery. Let us learn to say, however hard it may be, "Yes, Lord, if it is your will for me." The peace of God will rule in our hearts at least and the burden will become lighter. A burden accepted is half the burden borne. But the burdens we resist are always the heaviest. Whatever our burden let us cast it on the Lord and He will sustain us, be it the burden of our precious children who have strayed far from God and from us, or some more hidden sorrow of which the world knows nothing and about which the sufferer cannot unfold his bleeding heart to anyone, but must walk alone. What sorrow is there that is not known to the heart of God, and what person is there to whom God does not still say, "I have known your sorrow, I have heard your prayer and seen your tears"? Surely He mingles our sorrows with His own, for "He is a man of sorrows and acquainted with grief", and says to us, "Behold and see if there is any sorrow like unto my sorrow which is done unto me?" And so God speaks to us through the human lips and sorrows of Isaiah and Jeremiah, and He will speak through our sorrows to the world in which we live - not for our self-pity but for the salvation of others. Although we do not know how this can be, "the chastisement of our peace was upon him". The problem of human suffering is known to God alone, for it is His secret, but we do know that He Himself had to suffer in Jesus Christ His Incarnate Son more than any other ever had or could do. The Gospels tell us that the Jewish contemporaries of Jesus were blind and scorned the idea of a suffering Messiah as the Saviour of the world, but to us who are saved the sufferings of Christ were the unveiling of the heart of God and reveal something of His inexpressible Love for a world that has strayed far away from its Maker, a world gone mad in sin.

> *See! from his head, his hands, his feet,*
> *Sorrow and love flow mingled down;*
> *Did e'r such love and sorrow meet,*
> *Or thorns compose so rich a crown?"*

God calls us to love Him above all and to show our love by a blind trust in Him. To love and trust Him where we cannot see, where we cannot understand, "whom having not seen you love." As Job said, "Though he slay me yet will I trust him."

Apart from the Lord's call to us to accept what He chooses for us, or perhaps what He permits to come to us, there is another side to the problem of suffering. We often forget that we are in a world in which the Spoiler of God's creation is at work; he has not yet been cast out of the world, but is permitted to test and try the people of God. "The devil goes about", to quote St Peter again, "as a roaring lion seeking whom he may devour", but whom we are called "to resist steadfast in the Faith." We cannot understand what St. Paul called "the mystery of iniquity" that is at work in this present age, nor his statement that "He who now lets will let until he is taken out of the way." It is clear, however, that we are not to expect a life of ease, pleasure and comfort now. As one writer has written, "Let us take note of what the Good Shepherd does not promise. He assures us in all circumstances of His gracious presence and salvation, and of the gift of eternal life to us as we follow Him - but He does not promise us bread to the full, and rich clothing; nor does He promise us a peaceful and comfortable existence in the world according to our own standards." We can go on to recall that our Lord warned us that in the world we would have tribulation, that a man's enemies could be of his own household, that the lot of suffering must be part of the lot of those who follow Him all the way. Here we have no continuing city, for we seek a better country where God will wipe all tears away from our eyes and there will be no more pain or sorrow or death. The trouble is that we forget these promises and when trouble comes we are apt to resent it and rebel against it.

We learn in the Scripture that our misery is due in some way to the mystery of evil, but that Christ has already triumphed over the devil and all evil at the Cross. The resurrection of Christ assures us that there can be no doubt about that victory. The devil tried to turn our Lord away from the Cross, but He set His face steadfastly toward Jerusalem where in His death on the Cross sin was dealt its mortal blow. "Through death he destroyed him that had the power of death, that is the devil." The Cross and the Resurrection were the final victory of God's Love over all evil, and as such are the seal of our redemption. In them we have foretaste of our inheritance in Christ Jesus, and wait for its consummation at the end of the age. As the writer of the Epistle to the Hebrews reminds us, "Now we see not yet all things put under him. But we see Jesus, who was made a little lower than the angels, crowned with glory and honour, that he by the grace of God should taste death for every man." Thus the goal has already been won by the Captain of our salvation and is assured, so that we have, as it were, the title deeds already although the full possession of this wonderful inheritance is not yet manifest in the world. As someone has written: "The whole world so familiar and apparently so well established is tumbling around us, for God seems to be shaking, not the earth only, but the heaven itself." We are therefore not to be shaken by the adversities that overtake us, but are to hold on to our hope in God which is our "anchor, sure and steadfast within the veil".

Let us face the facts about the evil that abounds everywhere and attacks the Christians as well as non-Christians. It used to be thought sometimes in years gone by that if someone met with illness or calamity of any kind it was due to a secret sin or fault on his part. Even today some people seem to be inclined to think in this way. But that is surely a heathen idea. The inhabitants of the island of Malta where St Paul and his fellow travellers were shipwrecked drew that conclusion when Paul had gathered a bundle of sticks and laid them on the fire, and a viper came out of the heat and fastened on his hand. "When the barbarians saw the venomous beast hang on his hand, they said among themselves, 'no doubt this man is a murderer whom, though he has escaped the sea, yet vengeance does not suffer to live'." But St Paul shook off the viper and felt no harm.

Many of the greatest saints the world has ever seen have suffered great afflictions of body or mind, but out of whose sufferings there have come rivers of living water that brought health and life to many a spiritually distressed mind and soul. We can never judge a person's spirituality by the things that God permits to come into his life. The disciples of our Lord once asked Him about a man born blind, "Who did sin, this man or his parents that he should be born blind?" Jesus answered them as He would now answer many a distraught heart, "Neither has this man sinned, nor his parents, but that the works of God should be made manifest." "And this is the work of God", he said on another occasion," that you should believe on him whom the Father has sent." Any believer at any time may be called to suffer whether through his children or his family, whether in his own physical being or in his livelihood, in his business or in any way that touches the common life of man. No one will be exempt on account of his righteousness or his standing in Christ. No one can condemn or judge another, for the same thing can befall us all. We may often feel like the Psalmist when he cried out that heathen unbelievers did not seem to be plagued like other men! We should rather think that in their afflictions God is especially testing and trying the faith of His children. To use an Old Testament simile, He sits as a purifier of His children that when they are tested they may come forth as pure gold.

If we escape the criticism of our fellows there is still "the accuser of the brethren", as the devil was called. We are told in the Book of Revelation that the great "dragon was cast out; that old serpent called the devil and satan who deceives the whole world, was cast out on to the earth and his angels were cast out with him." "The accuser of our brethren is cast down who accused them day and night." But we also read that the people of God "overcame him by the blood of the Lamb, and by the word of their testimony; and they loved not their lives unto death." Who among Christians does not suffer from this arch-accuser? It seems to be his chief aim to attack the saints of God. At the least sin against conscience the false accuser is there to enlarge it and lie to us about our sin, and thus to make us so confused that we cannot tell what is conscience and what is the devil. Christian in Pilgrim's Progress tells of the time when he was attacked in this way. He heard such blasphemous words in his ears that he thought they came from his own heart, and was driven to despair until it was shown to him that they were the whisperings of the devil from outside of him. That is a true picture of what can take place, for the saints can still be tormented like that, through blaming themselves in various ways for what is not their own fault but is due to the devil himself who makes use of such occasions to hinder the faith of the saints. The devil may well have some truth in his accusations and that is why the poor Christian heart is so fearful, but he magnifies, distorts and twists it in such a clamouring and forceful way that one is beaten down before him. However, we recall that "they overcame him by the blood of the Lamb and the word of their testimony". Thank God there is a way of escape provided by our faithful God. "If we confess our sins he is faithful and just to forgive our sins and cleanse us from all unrighteousness", which He does through the blood of Christ. That precious blood of God's dear Son is our great provision in time of need and our haven of refuge from the accusations of the devil and all his angels. "Who shall lay anything to the charge of God's elect? It is God who justifies. Who is he that condemns? It is Christ that died, yea rather who is risen from the dead." Therefore the devil cannot prevail against us, for if we are redeemed and washed from our sins by the blood of Christ, then all the gates of hell cannot prevail against us. Therefore let us resist all the bombardment of evil that may beset us, for Christ is our Captain and Saviour now and for ever.

Many of God's people have been afflicted in this way for years, when the devil deluded them into thinking that they had committed the unpardonable sin, or brought upon themselves some special affliction. It turns the heart in upon itself through introspection and minute analysis of the self and its motives. A vicious circle is created from which the poor soul cannot find an outlet or relief. But the Word of God comes to the rescue, for He is the Sword of the Spirit - if we saturate ourselves in the Word of God until its language becomes imprinted on our heart, we will escape. "I, even I, am he who blots out all your transgressions, for mine own sake, and will not remember your sins." "I have blotted out as a thick cloud your sins: return unto me for I have redeemed you." "Thou wilt cast all their sins into the depths of the sea." That is the answer we throw back at satan when he accuses us, whether there be any truth in his accusations or not. We can confess our sins and be sure that the Lord will blot them all out, and we will be comforted. It is always the accusations of the devil that make every trial harder to bear. But let us remember what our Lord said to Peter, "Satan has desired to have you. But I have prayed for you that your faith may not fail." The Lord did not shelter Peter from the devil's accusations; He allowed him to be sifted by satan, but Peter was sustained by the assurance of Christ's own prayers which must always succeed and triumph over satan. This did not mean that Peter would never be at fault or that he would be perfect. We know that he denied the Lord, and recall how weak his faith was even in later years over the question raised by Judaising brethren about eating with the uncircumcised. And if tradition can be trusted, Peter sought at first to shun the death appointed for him, but then, as we know, he triumphed over all temptation and fought a good fight and won the crown of life. St Paul had not a little to say in his Epistles about the way in which Christian believers are assaulted by the devil, and so it was surely out of his own experience that he wrote to the Ephesians in plain language that we can understand: "Put on the whole armour of God that you may be able to withstand the wiles of the devil. For we wrestle not against flesh and blood, but against principalities, against powers, against the rulers of the darkness of this world, against spiritual wickedness in high places."

It is said or thought by so many these days that the idea of the devil is old fashioned and that there really is no devil at all. Nothing pleases the devil more than that! He desires that people should think of him as non-existent so that all evil may be laid at the feet of the saints especially. But satan is spoken of as the one "who deceives the whole world". Alas he also seeks to deceive the Church of our Lord Jesus Christ, and tries to make shipwreck of the faith of Christian people. But why should it be doubted? No one can get away from the fact that there is a certain insidious mystery of iniquity at work. What is the raging of one nation continuously against another but a manifestation of evil? What is the meaning of the depths of sin in our own country where so much is done for the moral well-being of the land? Not all the laws and attempts to stem the tide of wickedness can change the human heart or the nature of human society. Reforms can be carried out and succeed to an extent in transforming life, but the evil is still there. What about the unspeakable manifestation of evil that burst out among the Nazis with its utterly abominable murder of some six million Jews, not to speak of the devastating destruction brought upon mankind by Nazi war-mongering? And is not the growth of atheistic communism a mystery of iniquity? The devil has been at work deceiving the nations that there is no God and

The Straying Sheep—Faith Undaunted

has set his followers at work to produce a world without God and the Lord Jesus Christ. Atheistic communism is a masterpiece of the devil in our times. It is a religion without God and in spite of the moral claims for social well-being with which it cloaks itself, it develops an outlook antagonistic to all that is called God. What is the power behind it? For there is a power that sways peoples and nations, a power that strives to usurp the power of God and the Kingdom of Heaven. What is iniquity but an unseen evil force which is rampant everywhere and which is beyond the power of mankind to stamp out? It is a spiritual evil that stalks throughout the world seeking to wreck and overthrow all that God has created. There is nothing obsolete about this belief. There surrounds us on every side a dark world of wicked spirits, as St Paul remarked, and the evidence is clearly there for those who have eyes to see and the courage to face up to it. But however frightening it may be, the saints are kept by the power of God.

If, then, we consider these things as we face our hard spots in life, we shall find the difficulties appearing in a rather different light, for they are seen in the perspective of the conflict of the Kingdom of God with the forces of darkness. Our burden may actually grow lighter, for we find we are not alone in the struggle. Our young folk must learn to face the temptations of the world and the devil, and it is our part and our duty to share their difficulties in such a way as to take some of the burden on our own shoulders. Young people in their teens sometimes get very restless and find themselves caught up in an inner conflict which they cannot define and they dislike speaking about it. This calls for much patience and longsuffering on the part of their parents. But it is always best to let patience have its perfect work. I have heard women say in despair that everything they try to do by way of advice or suggestion seems to be taken wrongly and that the young people retaliate in heart-breaking ways. I remember one mother recounting how her teenage daughter had said "I am not going your way, and I don't want you to advise me". Her mother was an earnest Christian - what was she to do? One thing at least is necessary, not to force our parental opinions and ideas upon our children. It is easy for us to get irritated and to let ourselves go in such situations, but that is fatal and only makes the gap between us larger. If the Word of God had been taught in the proper way when the child was young, things might have turned out differently. It may have been, and yet it may not have been the case, but in any event it is no use looking back on the "might-have-beens". Some readjustment is now needed, and a new attitude toward the child will help. It does not do to show a defeatist attitude in the least. We must hold on to what we believe while trying to help our children, if they are so disposed, to believe in the same way as we do. For instance, they may be drawn by another denomination and come to prefer it. It is surely best for us to recognise their choice and not to insist on making them fit into our own pattern of worship. They may go to amusements or read books that we have no taste for. They long to dip into the world, and our hearts tremble with fear. I recall a lady saying once that her young son was becoming close friends with a girl that was not at all suitable through a physical handicap which could never be cured. But the more the mother was against it, the more he insisted on the friendship. They went to places together which were a sore trial to her. What should she do? It was quite evident that to be opposed openly to the friendship was driving them more and more together and to seek company elsewhere.

Sometimes God does let us have our own way and lets us burn our fingers, as it were, in doing things He really does not want us to do. When He sees us set on it He allows or seems to allow us to do what we want. Many of the Old Testament Psalms were evidently born out of situations of this kind. In the case of David who sinned in the matter of Uriah and Bathsheba God did allow David to halt for quite a long time until David had followed his own desires, while leaving God out of account. "I have gone astray like a lost sheep", said the Psalmist. God seems to let us stray into enemy terrain. He does not check us at once in the beginning of our wanderings. He could have prevented the Prodigal from departing into the far country, or the sheep from getting lost on the mountain. Our ways are ever before the Lord

The Straying Sheep—Faith Undaunted

and He knows just exactly when we take a step aside from His chosen paths for us. This is a mystery but it is sometimes His way of finding us. We will not own ourselves lost until we are on the brink of some catastrophe or have fallen into the miry clay or are in the slough of despair. These unhappy experiences are so often the very things that bring us back to Him. We are led astray for a while by our own inclinations and self-will, and not until they are exhausted will we turn back to Him. Sometimes our children too have to tread this road, carried along by some inward urge they can scarcely restrain.

There is a way for us all to take, and it is the way of Love. That is certainly God's way. We think of His patient love that followed us when we were young and rebellious and self-willed, when ambitions stirred in our breasts and the world beckoned us on to achieve them, and when perhaps even in our Christian life we still wanted to do things that our parents did not think wise and persisted in our headstrong will to try out our own way. What God has been to us we must try to be to our children. We are tempted of course, unlike God, to be overbearing and dictatorial in the face of opposition, but this will fail, for only love will prevail. Our Lord set much of this out in the Sermon on the Mount. Meekness, purity, mercifulness, peacemaking, and giving place to others, form the royal road. Not that we have to be puny Christians, but while holding tenaciously to our faith, we must beware lest our attitude toward those around us who are rebellious may provoke that rebellion further by our antagonism. Love can break down barriers that could never be dissolved in any other way. In the end it will be the Love of God that will smite the hearts of all who have rejected Him. There is no greater power in heaven or earth than love. Its power can break in pieces what nothing else can. Therefore love is our best and most potent weapon in the midst of these times of spiritual warfare. Let us as parents seek to bring ourselves into the fullness of the Love of God. That can only happen as we yield ourselves fully and completely to Him, keeping our gaze fixed upon Him in His Word until we are transformed into His likeness and look upon everything as He does. As He reigns supreme in our hearts we shall find much that distracts us melting away. In His Light we shall see light and we shall live so completely in Him that all we do or say will be the outflowing of His Love, and He will do for us and through us what we just cannot do for ourselves.

The enemy will try to get us down through our children, but we cannot be of any help to them that way. Some parents feel so ashamed of the doings of their children that they feel they ought to give up all Christian work and witness, but that is a temptation from the devil who wants us to do just that. We must go forward in patient well-doing, continuing our witness, cleaving to the Lord and leaving every issue in His hands. As we do so we shall find that the Lord will work for us in unexpected ways. It is the trial and test of faith and we must withstand the onslaughts of the devil. The prophet Habakkuk set us a fine example. He had to prophesy in the midst of what seemed the total ruin of his nation. God's wrath was poured out upon their persistent sins; through the cruelty of the Chaldeans - "that bitter people" - there took place the overthrow of all that had made Israel the chosen people of God, yet the prophet was undaunted in his faith. "For though the fig tree shall not blossom, neither shall fruit be in the vines; the labour of the olive shall fail, and the fields shall yield no meat; the flocks shall be cut off from the fold and there shall be no herd in the stalls: Yet I will rejoice in the Lord, I will joy in the God of my salvation." That is the faith that God wants from us, the faith of Abraham who against hope believed in hope, who staggered not at God's promises. That must also be our faith and it will come as we saturate ourselves with the Word of God. There is no limit to what faith can do.

We have to pray without ceasing. Prayer is the breath of life. It opens the spiritual lungs of our soul and enables us to take the deep breaths that we need so badly. God breathed into man and he became a living soul, and it is still by that breath of life that we must live, for without it we will wilt and perish. Prayer and the Word of God are our daily sustenance, but regular meals are needed, not spasmodic feeding on Him. The weakness of

The Straying Sheep—Faith Undaunted

Christians has often to do with the haphazard way in which they read the Word and pray. They do not regard it as vital, for they treat it as merely something extra rather than as arising out of a desperate need. There can be no strong vigorous Christian life unless these things have their right place in our daily affairs, in fact the chief place in our life. Prayer is perhaps the most difficult part of our service for the Lord. We lack the discipline that is needed to bring our whole body, soul and spirit into prayer as our Lord so strongly enjoined His disciples to do and in which He himself set the example, spending whole nights in prayer on the mountain top or in the garden alone with His Father. We are told how He offered up prayers with strong crying and tears and blood. If the Son of God while in the flesh on this earth was in such need of prayer, how much more do we need to engage in this kind of prayer that brings us into the presence of God? Surely prayer is required of all parents. We have to wrestle with God as Jacob wrestled with the angel at the brook Jabbok; until he was blessed by him, he would not let the angel go. That is the kind of prayer we must all brace ourselves to seek and to engage in. Great battles cannot be won by feeble effort, neither is it less possible to win them in the spiritual world unless we are in dead earnest.

The kind of prayer that prevails is the kind of prayer that is based on and steeped in the Word of God. We are not to present our own ideas and desires and plans, for we cannot advise God. He knows all before we ask but He waits to be gracious to those who seek Him "with all their heart". If we talk ourselves into the Word of God, if we accustom ourselves to think into the Word of God, if we draw from the Word of God our arguments and learn God's way, method and law in the spiritual realm, we shall then have the language of His Word put into our mouth, the mouth of our soul. There will be harmony in our prayer that cannot be if we are outside the knowledge of God given through His Word. All the great prayers of the prophets and the apostles, the fathers and the saints, were made on an approach to God with His own Word. They sought His face because of what He had promised to do for His people, for they were His people and He had assumed responsibility for them, while His great Name was at stake. Read what is recorded of Moses in Exodus thirty-four and at other places: how he pled for God's own Great Name among the heathen lest the heathen should say that God brought them out of Egypt but did not bring them in again from the wilderness. Again Moses pled with God on the ground of His promise to Abraham and the fathers and for the people's sake, because He said He loved them. Would God go back on His Word? In all these mighty prayers we are shown how to plead with God in prayer. Oh that we could get away from our puny selfish earth-bound prayers - the thing we call prayer! It was said on one occasion that the people perish from lack of knowledge. That could be said today. It is not enough to enjoy ourselves at special gatherings together, revelling in an exotic atmosphere of spiritual things. It will soon pass away like the vapour from a hothouse, but we need the rugged hard healthy prayer of the prophets who saw calamity coming upon people and the world. They kept God's purposes in view and thought of the on-coming crises as allowed by God to purge the world. It is so now. How blind so many of us are! How preoccupied in our own little corner, Church or circle! But all the time greater things are hovering over us as God overturns the world and calls us to wake up and watch and be ready to be "done with lesser things".

If then prayer is to prevail, it must be prayer that is in harmony with God and that corresponds with His revealed Will in the Scriptures. Do not divorce prayer from the Word of God; and that means the whole Word of God, not some choice passages here and there which we cull out of the Scriptures for our own selfish enjoyment. Everything in the Word applies to the whole Church, the whole Body of saints and the Kingdom of God. We certainly inherit the blessings individually but not just because we are separate individuals but because we are members of the glorious Body of Christ. Not a hair of our head shall perish without the Lord, but not because that is just you or I but because we are part of the whole and God knows the needs of His weaker members as well as of His others. We must be large in our prayers

The Straying Sheep—Faith Undaunted

and God will look on our smaller things. Prayer is not saying prayers; it is rather walking into and around Zion: "Go round about her, tell the towers thereof. Mark well her bulwarks, consider her palaces, that you may tell it to the generation following." Let us look at the mighty towers of strength that have been raised up by the saints before us, recall how they fought and won, how they raised up mighty bulwarks by prayer and how they hung their harps on the battlements of Zion that generations to come might see the mighty works wrought through prayer.

If we would win through for our young folk some of whom may be on the eve of wandering away from God, some of whom have already strayed far away, and some of whom have already been caught up in the wheels of the world, let us get down to real prayer and bombard God, as it were, with His own promises. Let us take the same words on our lips as Moses did, as Samuel did, and as a long train of saints who won on their knees through strong crying and prayer. Yet, let it be repeated, with God's own weapon - His Word. Our Lord's prayers were always prevailing because His will was one with the Father's. "I do always the things that please him". "As he has told me, so I speak." "As I live by the Father, so he who believes in me, he shall live by me." This is the only way to pray - to be in harmony with Christ our Lord, to do those things that are pleasing to Him and to have the Mind of Christ Jesus, as St Paul expressed it.

But "without faith it is impossible to please Him, for he who comes to God must believe that He is and that He is a rewarder of them that diligently seek him." So our prayer must always be the prayer of faith. We get this faith from the Word of God. As St Paul says, "Faith comes by hearing and hearing by the Word of God." As we hear God's Voice speaking through the written word to our hearts, faith will come and will grow. Faith and prayer depend on the Word of God. Apart from that, prayer is dead and there is no faith. We will always feel weak and impotent before the Lord, for such we are, but God knows that and has made provision for our imperfection. St Paul says in Romans eight, "The Spirit also helps our infirmities, for we know not what to pray for as we ought, but the Spirit himself makes intercession for us with groanings which cannot be uttered"; and, "He that searches the hearts knows what is the Mind of the Spirit, because He makes intercession for the saints, according to the will of God." The Father, the Son, and the Holy Spirit are all occupied with our prayers! Yet, the Lord desires to hear our prayers even though at best they are full of infirmities. There are times when we do not know what to ask yet the urge of prayer lies heavy upon us, and we groan in our need in a way that seems beyond our idea of speech. How blessed it is that we have the Holy Spirit who knows the will of God to pray for us and along with us.

Many years ago I went to prayer over a special request which seemed so urgent and which, had it been answered, would have altered the course of my own life at that time and that of my children. I felt the urge to return to the mission field. As I knelt in prayer with this deep urge upon me, I opened the Bible at these very verses in the Epistle to the Romans, and they held me. When I arose I knew my prayer had been answered completely in this matter, but it was not at all what I had thought or asked. The Holy Spirit took it in hand and He so convinced me that there was never any doubt that God had answered my prayer through the Holy Spirit quite apart from myself and answered it according to His will not mine. But with that answer came full satisfaction, rest, contentment, peace and joy. The years confirmed that the Holy Spirit did what was truly the Will of God, and there never was the slightest doubt from that wonderful moment. So the Holy Spirit is with us every step of the way if we believe. We pray for many things that are not His will, but with the refusal of our request or a different answer we shall be abundantly satisfied with His choice and shall rejoice that He knew best, and decided what was best. The issues were all with Him.

Beloved, as I close these meditations, some of which you may have heard before when we met together, let me say, Hold fast to the hope of salvation for your children. Never let it go. It is yours by right of God's gracious promise if you do your part. You may not see the answer in your day but God will answer in His own time and in His own way which will doubtless be different from what you thought. Surely faith implies this firmness in holding on and never letting go. We have been the means of bringing our children into the world and, in the language of St Paul, we may have to travail again for them in their spiritual birth. We have God on our side. Remember how He hovered over His people when they kept on rebelling against Him. Read Jeremiah and Isaiah in this light, and recall how the Lord said, "Oh Ephraim, shall I give you up?" How God pled for the return of His backsliding children in the early chapters of Jeremiah! God's heart is the perfect Parent's heart and you parents are in His company in this matter. He only knows the heart of a suffering parent and will He say "Nay" to His suffering children who in turn are parents? It is impossible. But we must cling on in faith like Abraham who staggered not but believed in hope against all hope and he won through. God blessed and honoured his faith, and so he will do now. Though we wait long years, though we may die without seeing the promises fulfilled now, nevertheless through faith we can see their fulfilment from far off, as the writer to the Hebrews says. So, as St. Paul says, let "Christ dwell in your hearts by faith; that being rooted and grounded in love, you may be able to comprehend with all saints what is the breadth and length and depth and height, and to know the love of Christ that passes knowledge, that you might be filled with all the fullness of God."

"Now unto him who is able to do exceeding abundantly above all that we ask or think, according to the power that works in us, unto him be glory in the church by Christ Jesus throughout all ages world without end. Amen."

www.ingramcontent.com/pod-product-compliance
Lightning Source LLC
Chambersburg PA
CBHW071331190426
43193CB00041B/1435